I0559349

The Founder's Journey

By

Paolo Narciso

Published by Hemingway publishers

Cover design by Hemingway publishers

ISBN: Printed in the United States

Preface

"The greatest danger for most of us is not that our aim is too high and we miss it, but that it is too low and we reach it. "

Michelangelo Buonarroti

"The biggest risk is not taking any risk. . . In a world that is changing quickly, the only strategy that is guaranteed to fail is not taking risks. "

Mark Zuckerberg

I welcome you on a transformational journey, one that will reshape not only your business but also yourself. This book is not just about becoming a CEO; it's about evolving into a leader who drives change, fosters innovation, and propels their company to unprecedented heights.

What Awaits You:

Imagine unlocking your full potential as a CEO, leading with unwavering confidence, and scaling your company beyond imagined limits. This book is a roadmap meticulously designed to guide you through a 12-week transformation. You will explore a holistic approach, bridging personal growth with strategic business acumen, to propel your company to new pinnacles.

The Journey that Led to This Book:

As I delved into the entrepreneurial landscape, I encountered countless driven individuals who had mastered the art of starting a business yet found themselves at a crossroads when it came to transitioning into the role of a CEO. I was one of those entrepreneurs. By the time I sold my second startup, because of the money I made for me and my investors, I could be labeled a success as a founder --- but not as a success as a CEO. In those years, I often questioned whether I was leading or simply managing. Was I truly solving the problems I sought out to solve? Was I the one who could truly scale this business? Meeting entrepreneurs grappling with the same fear of stagnation and the struggle to scale their businesses effectively fueled my resolve to pen down this comprehensive guide.

Picture this—a determined entrepreneur, much like yourself, pouring their heart and soul into their business, only to be held back by the challenges of leadership and growth. This book is my response to those whispers of uncertainty and the resolute drive to empower ambitious individuals like you to transcend these barriers.

Gratitude and Recognition:

I express profound gratitude to the unyielding spirit of entrepreneurs who dare to dream and act. Special acknowledgment goes to the mentors, colleagues, and individuals who shaped my journey and inspired the creation of this book. I can think of Tom Farrell, who helped me make the transition from a "tech guy" to a manager and then ultimately to a leader. John Sykes, the former CEO of Sykes Enterprises, gave me my first peek into how a founder of a small business ultimately scaled the business into a global leader with over 40,000 employees. Their wisdom and unwavering support have been invaluable in crafting this transformative guide, and for that, I am immensely thankful.

I also want to thank the entrepreneurs who let me interview them for my doctoral dissertation in 2016, which ultimately led to this book. I couldn't have done that project without the help and guidance of Drs John Lahm and Frank Lockwood of Western Carolina University. They were and continue to be my inspiration for the convergence of teaching and entrepreneurship in practice.

Lastly, I would like to thank my family and friends who have supported me throughout my own entrepreneurial journey. Being an entrepreneur can be the loneliest job on the planet. However, their support, love, and friendship have made the job worthwhile.

Invitation to a Transformative Experience:

To you, the entrepreneur with a fire in your belly and a vision in your heart, I extend a warm welcome to embark on this journey of evolution. Whether you're just stepping into the CEO role or seeking to redefine your leadership capabilities, this book is tailored to meet you where you are and guide you toward the heights you aspire to reach.

Who is this book for? This book is for the entrepreneur who hungers for growth, the visionary who craves transformation, and the leader who seeks to conquer new horizons. No prerequisite knowledge is required, only a willingness to learn, adapt, and lead with purpose. Thank you for choosing this book; let's continue this enlightening journey together.

How to read this book?

It may be odd to have a section that tells the reader how to read a book. I wrote this book to be relatively short. However, my suggestion is to read a chapter a week after Chapter 2. At the end of each chapter is a short "Putting It Into Practice" section. Take time to reflect on the questions in each of these sections. Write down your answers in a journal. Reflection is an essential skill that not only builds self-awareness but helps us to absorb and internalize what we learn.

Table of Contents

Chapter 1

The Power of Personal

Transformation

The early morning light filtered through the blinds in Evan's corner office, laying stripes of sunlight and shadow across the cherry wood desk. Today, the CEO of VisionTech found himself staring, not at the reports piled before him, but at the bustling cityscape several stories below. Evan's reflection—tired eyes, lined forehead—superimposed over the world he was trying to change.

Evan was beginning to understand that the journey to the peak of corporate leadership was intrinsically bound to the inner path of personal development. Keys to a kingdom of innovation and prosperity seemed of little use if one did not understand the doorway they were meant to unlock. He let out a sigh that carried the weight of his responsibilities and the eagerness to meet them better.

His thoughts turned towards his team, the individuals he was leading. Or was he simply managing? The distinction gnawed at him, demanding he distinguish between driving and nurturing growth. Somewhere between coaching sessions and strategic meetings, Evan realized the answer lay less in spreadsheets and more in the mirror.

The squeak of his CTO's running shoes on the hardwood floor broke his reverie. She placed a steaming cup of coffee next to his hand. The dark aroma promised alertness, but Evan found a deeper yearning surfaced—for clarity. He thanked her, eyes lingering on the mug's reflection.

The taste of the coffee was comfortingly bitter as the sounds of morning Slacks pinging softly in the background accompanied his contemplation. Evan recognized that his transformation and journey to true self-awareness would be the catalyst for the metamorphosis of VisionTech. The bellwether of transformation had to be intimately acquainted with his own fears and strengths to guide others effectively.

As Evan glanced at his Apple Watch, the minutes flipped closer to the hour. Another day was unfolding, one that held the promise for self-discovery and, in turn, the potential to spearhead company-wide innovation. But could he embrace this voyage of self as more than routine personal development? Could he allow it to become an odyssey that defined not only his leadership but the essence of his company's success?

Unleashing the CEO Within:
The Journey to Leadership Mastery

In an age where businesses evolve at breakneck speed, the linchpin of successful leadership lies not in tried-and-true playbooks or financial acumen but within the malleable depths of the CEO's own mindset. The traditional imagery of a CEO—stoic, distant, unfathomably assured—is being retired in favor of a leader who is reflective, dynamic, and, above all, personally transformed. **Chapter 1: The Power of Personal Transformation** serves as the bedrock of this revelation, promising to recalibrate your inner compass before setting sail toward business innovation and growth.

Understanding oneself, with all its quirks and potent potential, is the crystal-clear stream from which the wellspring of effective leadership flows. It's from this very introspection that a CEO discovers the capacity to inspire, guide, and elevate their organization. The conduit of personal growth to leadership competence is not wishful thinking but rather an empirically observable phenomenon. As we explore each new idea, we'll delve into the core concepts that spark this profound leadership transformation, fueling your journey from a passionate founder to a visionary CEO who can lead your company to new heights. In navigating this genesis of leadership, we lay down a path to create a mosaic of skills—hard and soft, bold and subtle—crafted through rigorous self-reflection and unwavering commitment to self-development.

Simultaneously, we outline the threads of continuity that weave through the entirety of **"CEO Evolution,"** ensuring that each chapter is a building block that complements and completes the grand design of your transformation. We will foray from the essence of a leadership metamorphosis to the tangible shift of mindset required in *Founder to CEO. The objective is to shift our mindsets, follow actionable steps and practical strategies for transformation, and then shape a strategic plan for success.*

The LEAD Model: A Blueprint for Transformation

The mosaic of extraordinary leadership is pieced together through a deliberate and well-structured structure approach we call the **LEAD Model**: a conceptual framework designed to support your progress from a self-aware executive to an empowered business pioneer.

Laying the Foundations with Self-Awareness

Beginning with **Self-awareness**, this model posits that an effective CEO must first be a student of their own character. Scrutinizing one's strengths, weaknesses, aspirations, and fears isn't simply self-analysis; it's the compass by which all strategic decisions and leadership styles are charted. Assessments and feedback loops serve as mirrors, reflecting not just the CEO you are but the potential you harbor within.

Educating Through Continuous Learning

The journey of a thousand miles, they say, begins with a single step—and that step is Continuous learning. The pursuit of knowledge is unending. Its path winds through workshops, literature, and the study of both triumph and failure. In this relentless journey of enlightenment, a CEO finds the innovative sparks to ignite business growth.

Amplifying Influence with Emotional Intelligence

In the forge of leadership, nothing tempers steel quite like Emotional Intelligence. As we go deeper into your internal reservoirs, we extract empathy—the ability to navigate not just your emotional depths but also those of your team. This component is a formidable tool, dictating the quality of relationships, the strength of collaboration, and the fabric of your organizational culture.

Defining Success with a Personal Leadership Style

Naturally arising from such inner work, developing a leadership style is a pursuit of authenticity. It's here that theory and introspection are refined into practical, personalized approaches to guiding a team, a department, or a business. In the alchemy of leadership, one's unique style is the philosopher's stone, transmuting base metal into gold.

Cultivating Support in Strong Networks

No CEO is an island, and Creating a Strong Support System acknowledges this truth. Surrounding oneself with mentors, peers, and champions isn't a sign of weakness but a hallmark of strength. Within this network, a CEO is not just bolstered but is also held accountable and inspired to reach ever-greater echelons of efficacy.

As the **LEAD Model** gains traction, its iterations become cyclical, fostering a CEO's evolution through a feedback loop that is as resilient as it is dynamic. The interaction between continuous learning and emotional intelligence, between self-awareness and leadership style, crafts a symphony of skills in tune with the needs of a burgeoning business.

The utility of this model reveals itself through its pragmatic approach. Businesses are living organisms, and in adapting the **LEAD Model**, a CEO equips them with the versatility to flourish in ever-shifting terrains.

Remember that the principles shared here are not merely abstract; they are a clarion call to action. They're a promise that within 12 weeks, by embracing personal transformation as the foundation, you will have started on the path to not just understanding these truths but living them—leading your business to soar without limits.

Understanding Personal Growth and Self-Awareness

In the fast-paced world of business leadership, the concept of personal growth often takes a back seat to profit margins and market share. However, as a CEO, who you are as a person significantly impacts your ability to lead. The journey to becoming an effective leader begins with a deep understanding of oneself. Self-awareness is the compass by which you can navigate through the challenges and opportunities of leading a company. Without it, you risk being adrift in a sea of external factors dictated by the tides of the market rather than your own values and vision.

Effective leadership starts with self-awareness and personal growth. CEOs must take responsibility for their own emotional intelligence and personal development before they can successfully foster growth within their organization. Without a deep understanding of their own strengths, weaknesses, and unique perspectives, their efforts may be inconsistent or even counterproductive.

Successful leadership requires a strong foundation of self-knowledge. By taking the time to reflect on their own capabilities, limitations, and viewpoints, CEOs can identify areas for personal growth and development. This introspection allows them to cultivate the qualities and skills necessary for effective leadership, such as emotional intelligence, adaptability, and strategic thinking.

Only when CEOs have a firm grasp on their own personal growth can they effectively guide their organization towards success. By prioritizing their own emotional intelligence and personal development, they lay the groundwork for consistent, impactful leadership that drives positive change and fosters a culture of growth within their company. There's evidence to support the notion that self-awareness is linked to heightened emotional intelligence, better decision-making, and improved leadership abilities. Research published in the **Harvard Business Review** suggests that leaders who have strong self-awareness are often more effective and have more profitable companies. What's key to understanding is that personal growth is not a destination; it's a continual process that feeds into every decision you make and every relationship you manage, both inside and outside the boardroom.

To further complicate matters, there's no one-size-fits-all map for personal development. It requires a tailored approach, one that involves regular self-reflection, seeking feedback, and committing to mindful changes in behavior. It's about recognizing that the path to becoming a great CEO isn't solely about market analysis and strategic investments; it's equally about personal introspection and growth.

The essence of leading a successful company stems from leading oneself first, with self-awareness and personal growth as the bedrock of effective leadership.

Cultivating Leadership Skills through Self-Reflection and Development

As much as business is about numbers, it's also about people — and being a leader is fundamentally about relationships. To steer those relationships in a positive direction, a CEO must first look inward. Leadership skills, akin to complex machinery, require routine maintenance and fine-tuning through self-reflection and personal development. It's about honing your capabilities not only as a business strategist but as a compassionate, effective communicator and listener.

How often do we pause and reflect on our interactions with others? Self-reflection gives us the mirror we need to understand our impact on those around us. It helps us identify patterns in our behavior that may be contributing to or hindering our effectiveness as leaders. For instance, are you truly listening to your team members' ideas? Do you inspire them to take on new challenges? These questions dig at the root of what it means to lead.

Leadership development programs often stress the importance of continuous learning. A leader's education never truly ends. Each new experience, each mistake, is an opportunity to absorb a lesson that can refine your leadership skills. So, keep a journal, set aside time for reflection, and challenge yourself to grow from every situation.

Empathy and humility are marks of great leaders. They understand that they do not lead in a vacuum but within a dynamic environment full of unique individuals. How does your leadership touch the lives of others? By reflecting deeply on and developing your emotional intelligence, you strengthen your ability to influence, motivate, and connect with your team.

Driving Innovation and Growth Through Personal Transformation

Innovation doesn't come from sitting still or maintaining the status quo. It springs from the well of personal transformation and the pursuit of self-improvement. Leaders who are committed to their own growth are better equipped to foster a culture of innovation within their companies. Just like a tree cannot bear fruit without strong roots, a company cannot reach the heights of industry leadership without a firmly grounded and growing CEO.

Consider a sculptor chiseling away at a block of marble. She must first understand the properties of the stone — its resilience, its veins, and its potential from within. Similarly, you must understand the strengths and vulnerabilities within yourself to carve out innovation in your business effectively. An intimate knowledge of your own passions, values, and creative process will guide the strategic choices you make, choices that can stand as pillars of innovation in your company.

The statistics are clear: Companies led by visionary leaders who consistently challenge themselves are more likely to push boundaries and grow. Their personal transformation serves as a catalyst, not only for their own development but for their entire organization. By embracing change, showing vulnerability, and leading by example, you inspire your employees to do the same.

Incorporate novel practices into your self-improvement routine. This could mean learning from other industries, embracing failures as learning opportunities, or simply stepping out of your comfort zone. It is through these practices that you can foster a more innovative and resilient business.

Connecting the dots between personal transformation, leadership skill development, and business growth reveals a clear picture. It shows that the very qualities that define you as a person are the same ones that can elevate your company to new heights. Embrace the power of personal transformation to forge the future of your business.

Now, consider these thoughts. Where in your self-reflection could you find the seeds of innovation that your company needs? Can personal transformation truly be the key to unlocking a new paradigm of leadership and growth?

I hope you now see the incredible power and potential that lies within the personal transformation. **Understanding the importance of personal growth and self-awareness** is not just a luxury for CEOs; it is a necessity. As you reflect on these ideas, remember that your journey of personal growth is not just about becoming a better leader; it's about discovering the untapped potential within yourself and your company. By embarking on this path of self-discovery, you'll uncover new ways to innovate, inspire, and drive your business forward. The power to transform your company lies within you—all you need to do is take the first step.

Cultivating leadership skills through self-reflection is not a one-time task but a continuous process of growth and refinement. Remember, leadership is not just about directing others; it's about inspiring, guiding, and empowering those around you. As you delve deeper into your own leadership style, you're setting yourself up to lead with authenticity and purpose.

Lastly, **establishing a solid foundation for driving innovation and growth** within your company starts with you. Your personal transformation will ripple outwards, influencing the culture and trajectory of your entire organization. By focusing on your own growth, you are igniting a spark that has the potential to ignite revolutionary change within your business.

As we conclude this introductory chapter, I invite you to embark on a transformative journey that will redefine your leadership and propel your business to new heights. The insights and strategies you'll discover in the coming chapters will equip you with the tools to unleash your full potential as a visionary CEO. From mastering the art of empowering leadership to developing practical strategies for transformation and crafting a strategic plan for success, each chapter builds upon the foundation of personal growth and self-awareness we've explored here.

But knowledge alone is not enough; it's the application of these principles that will truly set you apart as a leader. That's why each chapter concludes with a "Putting It Into Practice" section, providing you with actionable steps and exercises to integrate these concepts into your daily life and leadership approach. By committing to this process of self-reflection, continuous learning, and personal development, you'll not only transform yourself but also inspire and guide your team to achieve extraordinary results.

So, are you ready to unlock the full potential of your leadership and drive innovation and growth like never before? The next chapters are designed to be your blueprint for success, offering you a step-by-step guide to becoming the visionary leader your company needs. By dedicating yourself to this transformative process, you'll unlock the full potential of your leadership and drive innovation and growth like never before. Your evolution as a CEO starts now, and the impact you'll make on your business and the lives you touch will be nothing short of remarkable. Embrace the power of personal transformation and prepare to lead your company to unprecedented success.

Chapter 2

Founder to CEO: Shifting Mindsets

Amid the unmistakable hum of the bustling coffee shop, where the aroma of freshly ground beans waged a gentle war against the scent of rain clinging to coats and umbrellas, Eliza wrestled silently with the weight of transformation. The worn leather of the booth beneath her whispered stories of countless others who had sat pondering life's turning points. She, now on the cusp of trading the safety of a founder's dream for the unexplored realm of a CEO, felt a tug in his gut. Her thoughts drifted like steam from her cup, recounting conversations with mentors and the tapestry of advice woven through them.

A quiet clink of ceramic disrupted her reverie. The waiter's smile, undimmed by the day's gloom, anchored her back to the present. She nodded in thanks, his presence a temporary buoy in the sea of her concerns. Outside, gray clouds lumbered across the sky, indifferent to the turmoil within Eliza's chest. Such a reflective struggle, she realized, could not be discerned by casual observers. It was a solitary journey, changing who you had to be, leaving behind the comforts of what you once were.

The early victories of her venture reeled through her memory, each one sweet and piercing in its clarity. They were seeds sown with passion and watered with relentless drive; each sprout was a testament to her capacity to create. But creation was no longer her sole duty. There lay before her an expanse where she must grow, evolve, and lead not just in bursts of invention but through the steady rhythm of decision and direction. This was no longer the playground of ideas; it was the battlefield of execution.

She took a bite from her sandwich, the crunch of the lettuce grounding and the simplicity of the meal, which was a stark contrast to the complexity of her thoughts. It seemed absurd, the contrast between the ordinary act of eating and the extraordinary transition that loomed ahead. She silently rehearsed speeches she might give, the faces of her team flickering in her mind's eye. How do we convey this shift? How to inspire them to join her in this leap into uncharted waters?

Setting her cup down, Eliza felt a sudden surge of resolve. Aesthetic came less from the grandeur and more from the quiet moments of decision, the unspoken promise to oneself to venture into discomfort for the sake of something greater. In this quiet corner, with the rain whispering against the windows and the world outside oblivious, she embraced the daunting path that stretched before her.

Did she possess the fortitude to transcend the founder's mindset and mold herself into a leader of the future legacy? Would she recognize herself once she'd done so? And for every Eliza perched on the cliff of transformation, might there be a silent symphony of resolve playing within?

Embrace the Shift: From Visionary to Vision Executor

The journey from founding a startup to steering it as a CEO represents one of the most profound transitions in the entrepreneurial world. This movement is more than a simple role change; it demands a complete overhaul in mindset—a leap from the hands-on, gritty culture of startup life to a strategic, leadership-oriented approach. Boarding on this path requires a driven individual to recognize the fundamental shift in perspective that is essential when moving from the founder's seat to the CEO's office. The ability to adapt, grow, and scale a business hinges on this critical transformation.

The transition is not merely about broadening one's skill set but about embracing a new identity. A founder is typically engrossed in product development, market fit, and perhaps the initial stages of customer acquisition. However, a CEO's responsibilities stretch far and wide, involving strategic decision-making, leadership, culture building, and ensuring the company's financial health. This leap necessitates a breakthrough in thinking, allowing innovation to guide not only product development but also company-wide strategy, employee engagement, and business development.

Key to this transformation is a commitment to continuous learning. The journey from founder to CEO is unchartered for many, fraught with challenges and learning curves. A groundbreaking CEO is a lifelong learner who views hurdles as opportunities to grow, diving into advanced education, seeking mentorship, and engaging in diverse educational journeys. This drive for knowledge is fueled by the desire to make a difference, not just within the company but also in the wider community, empowering teams and addressing the needs of underserved communities.

Stepping out of one's comfort zone is another pivotal aspect of the transition. It requires a mental rewire to adopt a mindset focused on leading a company towards scalable success. The vision founders hold dear must evolve from being a personal mission to a shared vision, one that inspires and mobilizes an entire organization. This step is critical in scaling operations, engaging stakeholders, and ensuring the company's longevity and impact.

Recognizing the need for a changed mindset opens the door to unlocking one's full potential as a CEO. It is not enough to be a visionary; one must also become a vision executor. This involves adopting a strategic approach to leadership, focusing on how to empower and leverage the talents of a growing team, developing effective marketing strategies, and making data-driven decisions to lead the company towards sustainable growth and breakthrough success.

Engaging in this evolutionary process also means accepting the responsibility to drive not just business growth but social innovation as well. As said above, A successful CEO is one who can scale their company while making significant contributions to society, whether by addressing societal issues through innovative products or services or by creating a company culture that prioritizes social responsibility.

Your Path to Transformation

Recognizing the fundamental shift from founder to CEO is essential because it impacts every decision a CEO makes, from strategic planning to daily operations. A founder might concentrate on product development or market entry strategies driven by passion and a deep understanding of the product. A CEO, on the other hand, needs to balance this with considerations of company culture, long-term sustainability, shareholder value, and more. This doesn't mean losing the founder's visionary zeal but augmenting it with a more nuanced understanding of the business as a whole.

The mental shift also involves embracing a more analytical approach towards problem-solving and decision-making. Where a founder may have relied heavily on intuition and personal conviction, a CEO benefits from a more data-driven approach. This change doesn't diminish the importance of gut feeling but places it within a broader, more comprehensive framework of business intelligence and strategic analysis.

Such a transformation can be challenging. It requires not just acquiring new skills but reshaping one's identity and self-perception within the business. This process is crucial for personal growth and the company's success. It is a time of profound learning, unlearning, and relearning—a period that, while demanding, is immensely rewarding.

Transitioning from founder to CEO requires embracing a comprehensive view of leading a company, moving beyond the product to contemplate the broader business landscape.

Embrace New Challenges and Commit to Continuous Learning

Adopting a CEO's mindset is like stepping into a rapidly flowing river. The current is strong, and the waters are constantly changing. To navigate this environment, embracing new challenges and committing to continuous learning are non-negotiable. This environment is fast-paced, highly competitive, and ever-changing, demanding a mindset that views challenges as opportunities to learn and grow rather than as obstacles.

Continuous learning is the cornerstone of leadership development. It is not merely an academic pursuit but a practical, life-long commitment to personal and professional growth. For a CEO, this encompasses not just business-related knowledge but also an understanding of global economic trends, technological advancements, and even the psychology of leadership and team dynamics. This wide-ranging knowledge base empowers CEOs to make informed decisions, anticipate market changes, and lead their companies with confidence.

Embracing new challenges involves a willingness to step outside one's comfort zone. It means engaging with unfamiliar situations, being open to feedback, and experimenting with new strategies. Each of these opportunities is a chance to learn something new about the business, the team, or oneself. This approach fosters a culture of innovation within the company, as employees see leadership valuing curiosity and resilience.

Commitment to continuous learning and getting your hands on new challenges are traits that mark successful CEOs. They understand that the landscape of business is perpetually evolving and that staying ahead requires a proactive, learning-oriented mindset. This dedication to growth is not just about acquiring knowledge but about applying it effectively to navigate the complexities of leading a successful company.

What if viewing each new challenge as a learning opportunity is the key that unlocks your full potential as a CEO?

Step Out of Your Comfort Zone

The journey from founder to CEO is marked by a series of transitions out of comfortable territories into realms that test one's limits and capacities. It's similar to a climber who, after mastering the familiar trails of their home mountain, decides to tackle Everest. This leap requires not just physical readiness but a mental shift—the willingness to face unknown challenges, learn from them, and push beyond previous boundaries.

To lead a company towards success, adopting a mindset that accepts, indeed welcomes, discomfort as a growth opportunity is essential. This is not about reckless risk-taking but about thoughtful exploration of new strategies, technologies, and business models that can drive the company forward. It means engaging with changes in the market with curiosity and seeing them as a chance to innovate and differentiate.

This mindset encourages a culture of resilience and adaptability within the company. When employees see their leaders stepping confidently into new challenges, they are more likely to embrace change themselves. This cascading effect can transform the entire organization, making it more agile and better equipped to navigate the uncertainties of the business world.

Stepping out of your comfort zone and adopting a mindset aligned with leading a company towards success involves embracing change, pursuing continuous learning, and viewing challenges as opportunities for growth.

Embrace the challenges and dilemmas that come with leading a company. Approach each obstacle as an opportunity to learn and grow. Stay committed to expanding your knowledge and honing your skills. **By adopting a mindset of a continuous learner, you position yourself for insightful decision-making and impactful leadership**. Look beyond your comfort zone for innovation and explore new avenues to propel your company forward.

Strive for Extraordinary Success

Step out of your comfort zone and boldly embrace the CEO role. This shift demands a strategic mindset, a keen eye for business development, and a passion for leading with purpose. **By aligning your goals with scaling your company and empowering those around you**, you set the stage for extraordinary success. Welcome the challenges, leverage your expertise in strategy and marketing, and lead your company towards a future where your vision transforms into reality.

Putting It Into Practice

Now that you've explored the connection between personal growth and business success, it's time to start your own journey of self-discovery and transformation. Use the following prompts and exercises to guide you:

1. **Reflect on your leadership style:**
- What are your strengths as a leader?
- In what areas do you see room for improvement?
- How can you leverage your unique qualities to inspire and motivate your team?

2. **Identify your personal growth opportunities:**
- What skills or knowledge gaps do you want to address?
- Are there any limiting beliefs or behaviors holding you back?
- How can you step outside your comfort zone to experience growth?

3. **Develop a personal growth plan:**
- Set specific, measurable goals for your personal development.
- Break these goals down into actionable steps and create a timeline for achievement.
- Consider seeking guidance from a mentor, coach, or trusted advisor.

4. **Foster a growth mindset within your organization:**

- Lead by example, sharing your own growth journey with your team.
- Encourage continuous learning and development at all levels of your company.
- Create a culture that values innovation, experimentation, and learning from failure.

5. **Regularly assess and adjust your plan:**

- Schedule time for self-reflection and evaluation of your progress.
- Celebrate your successes and learn from your setbacks.
- Adapt your plan as needed to ensure continued growth and alignment with your goals.

Remember, personal transformation is an ongoing process, not a one-time event. By committing to your own growth and development, you'll not only become a more effective leader but also inspire others to do the same. Embrace the journey, trust the process, and watch as your company thrives under your visionary leadership.

Chapter 3

Empowering Leadership

The morning light had begun its steady crawl across Jessica Lenz's polished mahogany desk. Sun rays danced with the drifting dust, a silent waltz witnessed only by the inanimate and her deep, contemplative eyes. The office around her was uncluttered, save for a framed photo of her team on the credenza, her champions of ingenuity. As the CEO of Innovatech Solutions, she held the steering wheel of the company's future, yet Jessica knew that the true drivers were her people.

Today's agenda held a weight that pressed against her chest. It was a delicate day of decision. For weeks, a malaise had taken root within the vibrant start-up she crafted from the ground up. Morale had dipped; whispers of uncertainty had threaded through the open-plan floor below where ideas used to bloom like wildflowers. She felt the pulse of the problem but hesitated to prescribe a remedy before its cause revealed itself to her.

Lines of concern sketched across Jessica's forehead as she recollected a past frigid with similar challenges. The memory of old failures, like specters, clawed at the edges of her resolve. Had she not learned from the time when she bore the weight alone, believing leadership was a tower, solitary and unassailable? The echo of that fall from hubris still rang in her ears.

She leaned forward, resting her elbows on the desk, inhaling deeply. Within her, a voice stirred, reminding her of the collaborative symphony she once conducted effortlessly. It whispered secrets of empowerment and the unmatched strength found in collective aspiration. Jessica envisioned a workplace buoyant with trust and vibrant discussion, where every voice carved the path forward.

The door to her office clicked softly open, and Sarah, her lead product developer, peered in tentatively. "Morning, Jess. Got a minute?"

"Always," Jessica replied her voice the calm eye of the storm. Sarah stepped in, apprehension painting her features. This was it—the living embodiment of Jessica's current test. She listened, truly listened, as Sarah spoke of hidden frustrations among the team, of the stifling of their creative heart.

Together, they talked, ideas and challenges laid bare on Jessica's desk like a map to be navigated by two captains instead of one. They spoke of leadership as if it were not a summit to be conquered but a tide to be ridden, and it was not the CEO's sole terrain but the shared sea of every crew member aboard this venture.

Sarah's worries began to deflate, replaced by something lighter, something hopeful. Jessica noticed this subtle transformation, drawing a parallel to the shift within herself. They parted with a plan of action, a seed planted in fertile soil.

The office was still, yet the tableau had shifted. There were no grand epiphanies, but a thread had been woven tighter into the tapestry of their company culture. Jessica gazed at the team photo once more. Her mind buzzed with the upcoming changes. Would the team rally once they realized their own strength and voice? Or perhaps the real question lingered in the space between, where the next leader might unearth their latent potential, reshaping the fabric of Innovatech Solutions one empowered decision at a time.

Transforming Vision into Action: The Power of Empowering Leadership

In the journey from founder to CEO, understanding the essence of true leadership is indispensable. Leadership is inherently about fostering an environment where each team member can flourish, innovating together towards a shared vision. It's a myth that successful CEOs need to be omniscient or the quintessential genius in the room. Instead, **true leadership is characterized by the ability to empower others**, to encourage collaboration, and to leverage the collective strengths and diversity of the team to achieve breakthrough results.

Effective leadership instills a sense of ownership and agency among team members, enabling them to contribute their best work. By prioritizing empowerment, visionary CEOs create a fertile ground for cutting-edge ideas and revolutionary solutions to emerge. It's about making a difference by harnessing the power of collaboration, innovation, and strategic foresight. This approach is not just beneficial; it's crucial for scaling a business and fostering a culture that's committed to excellence and continuous improvement.

Nurturing a collaborative environment requires a shift in perspective. Moving away from traditional top-down management models to a more inclusive leadership style can seem daunting at first. However, the rewards are immeasurable. Leaders who focus on empowering their team members find themselves at the helm of an engaged, motivated, and highly productive workforce. This chapter aims to guide you on how to accomplish this paradigm shift, focusing on **leveraging the strengths of your team** to create an enduring culture of cooperation and innovation.

To drive sustainable growth, it's essential to engage every member of your team in the process. This entails creating platforms for open communication, encouraging risk-taking within safe boundaries, and providing opportunities for personal and professional development. Empowering leadership is about being a catalyst for change, fostering an environment where everyone feels valued and heard. It's about scaling not just the operations of your business but also the aspirations and capabilities of your team.

This transformation doesn't happen overnight. It's a journey that requires commitment, resilience, and a willingness to learn and adapt. As you transition from founder to CEO, embracing the role of an empowering leader will equip you to overcome challenges and seize opportunities with confidence. You will learn to build a cohesive, innovative team that is driven to achieve and surpass your business goals.

Driving sustainable growth hinges not merely on strategic planning and market analysis but significantly on the empowerment of your team. By concentrating on enabling and empowering your team members, you orchestrate a shift towards a more agile, resilient, and innovative organizational culture. This shift is instrumental in navigating the complexities of scaling a business in today's fast-paced, competitive landscape.

By the end of this chapter, you should be equipped with the knowledge and tools to cultivate a culture that values cooperation, innovation, and shared leadership. Remember, the journey from founder to CEO is also a personal transformation—one that requires you to continually evolve your leadership style to meet the changing needs of your business and your team. Empower your team, and watch as they propel your business to new heights, breaking through barriers and achieving unprecedented success.

Understand that Effective Leadership is About Empowering Others and Fostering Collaboration

Empowerment and collaboration are not just buzzwords; they are fundamental components for cultivating a thriving workplace. When leaders empower their teams, they enable them to take ownership of their responsibilities and contribute their best efforts towards the organization's goals. Such an environment is not only conducive to innovation but also builds a resilient culture that can navigate challenges more effectively.

Imagine leadership as gardening. The gardener doesn't grow the plants but creates the conditions for growth. They ensure the soil is fertile, there's enough sunlight, and the plants are watered regularly. Similarly, influential leaders create the conditions where team members can flourish. They provide the necessary resources, guidance, and support but allow the individual's capabilities to drive their growth.

However, this requires trust—a commodity that's earned over time. Trust is the foundation upon which empowerment is built. Without it, efforts to delegate and encourage autonomy can falter. Leaders demonstrate their trust in their teams by giving them the freedom to make decisions and by valuing their input. This, in turn, fosters a collaborative environment where diverse ideas and perspectives combine to create innovative solutions.

The crucial role of a leader is to empower and collaborate, creating a fertile ground for innovation and growth.

Learn How to Leverage the Strengths of Your Team and Create a Culture of Innovation and Cooperation

The success of any organization hinges on its ability to leverage the diverse strengths of its team members. Every individual brings a unique set of skills, knowledge, and experiences to the table. Recognizing and utilizing these disparate strengths is a hallmark of astute leadership. This approach not only maximizes the organization's potential but also enhances the job satisfaction of its members, as they feel valued and understood.

Creating a culture of innovation and cooperation starts with embracing the notion that great ideas can come from anywhere within the organization. It requires a shift from a top-down directive to a more inclusive and collaborative approach. Leaders must cultivate an environment where every voice is heard and each team member feels empowered to contribute. This democratic ethos is the breeding ground for cutting-edge ideas and breakthrough solutions.

Communication and transparency are key to fostering this culture. Open lines of communication ensure that ideas can be shared freely and without fear of judgment. Transparency about goals, challenges, and failures builds trust and encourages a shared sense of purpose. Together, these elements create a cohesive team that can tackle complex problems more effectively.

Consider a symphony orchestra as an analogy. In an orchestra, each musician plays a unique instrument that contributes to the overall harmony. The conductor's role is not to play every instrument but to understand each one's contribution and guide the musicians toward a mesmerizing performance. Similarly, a leader must recognize each team member's strengths and how they can harmonize to achieve the organization's vision.

However, leveraging these strengths and creating a culture of innovation doesn't happen overnight. It requires deliberate efforts, consistent practice, and a commitment to personal growth and development both for the leader and the team. It's a journey of transformation that leads to a more agile, resilient, and innovative organization.

Could understanding and embracing the unique strengths of each team member be the key to unlocking unprecedented innovation and cooperation in your organization?

Drive Sustainable Growth and Success Within Your Company by Focusing on Enabling and Empowering Your Team Members

Sustainable growth is the Holy Grail for any organization. Yet, achieving and maintaining it requires more than just strategic planning and financial investment. It necessitates empowering your team members to contribute their best, enabling them to innovate and adapt in an ever-changing business landscape.

Enabling and empowering your team starts with a commitment to their professional and personal growth. Investing in their development not only equips them with the skills needed to excel in their roles but also signals that you value them as integral parts of the organization. This, in turn, fosters loyalty, increases engagement, and drives productivity, laying a solid foundation for sustainable growth.

Empowered employees are more likely to take initiative, anticipate and solve problems, and seek continuous improvement in their work. They feel a sense of ownership and responsibility towards the organization's success, which motivates them to go the extra mile. Furthermore, when employees are empowered, they bring diverse perspectives and creative solutions to the table, driving innovation and keeping the organization ahead of the curve.

Empowerment and enabling your team, therefore, are not just strategies but cornerstones of a culture that celebrates contribution, recognizes effort, and values innovation. This culture not only attracts top talent but also retains it, making the organization resilient and adaptable amidst challenges.

Empowering and enabling your team members are the bedrock of building a culture that supports sustainable growth and success. **By investing in your team's growth, fostering their sense of ownership, and leveraging their diverse strengths, you position your company to thrive in the face of perpetual change.**

Empowering Leadership at the Core of Success

Effective leadership is not about having all the answers but empowering others. **By fostering collaboration and leveraging the strengths of your team, you can create a culture that thrives on innovation and cooperation.** The true essence of leadership lies in enabling your team members to reach their full potential and collectively drive the company toward success. **It's not about being the smartest person in the room but about harnessing the collective intelligence and expertise within your organization.**

Driving Sustainable Growth Through Empowerment

As a leader, your focus should be on empowering and enabling your team rather than micromanaging or dictating. Embrace the uniqueness and talents of each individual in your team, allowing them to excel in their strengths. **By doing so, you can unlock a level of creativity and collaboration that propels your company towards sustainable growth and success. Remember, it's not about doing it all but about creating an environment where each member can contribute meaningfully.**

A Culture of Innovation and Cooperation

Creating a culture of innovation and cooperation is fundamental to the long-term success of your company. Encouraging your team to think outside the box, experiment with new ideas, and collaborate seamlessly can lead to breakthrough results. Embrace diversity of thought and celebrate varied expertise within your team, as this is where truly revolutionary ideas are born. As a leader, your role is to facilitate this environment and enable your team to achieve unparalleled levels of success.

Putting It Into Practice: Empowering Your Team for Success

Now that we have discussed enough about becoming an empowering leader, it's essential to put the concepts into action. Use the following exercises and reflection prompts to guide you in creating a culture of collaboration, innovation, and empowerment within your organization.

1. **Assess your current leadership style:**
   - Reflect on how you currently lead and interact with your team.
   - Identify areas where you can improve in terms of empowerment and collaboration.
   - Consider seeking feedback from your team to gain insights into your leadership approach.

2. Foster open communication and transparency:

- Establish regular check-ins and open forums for your team to share ideas and concerns.
- Practice active listening and create a safe space for everyone to contribute.
- Be transparent about company goals, challenges, and decision-making processes.

3. Identify and leverage the strengths of your team members:

- Take time to understand the unique skills, experiences, and perspectives each team member brings.
- Assign roles and responsibilities that align with individual strengths and passions.
- Encourage team members to share their knowledge and expertise with others.

4. Empower your team to take ownership and make decisions:

- Delegate tasks and projects that challenge and develop your team members' skills.
- Provide the necessary resources, guidance, and support for them to succeed.
- Encourage calculated risk-taking and learning from failures.

5. **Invest in your team's growth and development:**

- Offer opportunities for training, mentoring, and professional development.

- Support your team members' career aspirations and help them create growth plans.

- Lead by example and commit to your own continuous learning and growth.

6. **Celebrate successes and recognize contributions:**

- Acknowledge and appreciate the efforts and achievements of your team members.

- Share success stories and highlight how collaboration and innovation drove results.

- Create a culture of recognition and appreciation that motivates and inspires your team.

7. **Continuously evaluate and adapt your leadership approach:**

- Regularly assess the impact of your empowering leadership style on your team and organization.

- Seek feedback from your team and be open to constructive criticism.

- Adapt your approach as needed to meet the evolving needs of your team and business.

Remember, becoming an empowering leader is an ongoing journey. It requires consistent effort, self-reflection, and a willingness to learn and grow. By putting these practices into action and making empowerment a core part of your leadership philosophy, you'll create a thriving, collaborative, and innovative culture that drives sustainable success for your organization.

Chapter 4

Practical Strategies for Transformation

The morning light filtered through the expansive windows of the corner office, casting a warm glow on the mahogany desk that stood as a testament to the success of a business empire. Alexander Chase, the CEO of an innovative tech company, sat rigidly in his leather chair, his gaze fixed outside where the city pulsed with a rhythm of a different kind — one of unforgiving competition and relentless change. The skyscrapers reached for the heavens, a mere backdrop to the storm brewing in Alexander's mind.

He knew leadership was not merely about analytical prowess or strategic acumen; it was an art that demanded the deft balance of mind and emotion, and of late, Alexander felt his balance waver. As his fingers tapped a staccato rhythm on the desk, his thoughts drifted to the leadership seminar he had attended the week before, where the idea of 'CEO Evolution' had struck him like a lightning bolt — the synthesis of effective tactics and profound psychological shifts.

In the breath of his office, where whispers of ambition and legacy hung heavily in the air, he could feel the weight of his own resistance. He'd mastered the elements of business, but the elusive subtleties of emotional intelligence and effective communication — these were terrains he had yet explored to their full depths. Such deficits had cost him dearly in the past — a promising partnership dissolved, a misunderstood directive, the morale of his team shaken by his unintentional brusqueness.

Alexander's hand brushed against the smooth leather of the chair, its texture grounding him as he recalled the sharp words of the seminar's speaker, "The tools of leadership are molded in the kiln of self-awareness and sharpened on the stone of genuine interaction. " He knew it was time for a transformation, not just of his business, but of himself as its leader.

As the sun climbed higher, casting long shadows across the room, Alexander pondered how he might integrate these new strategies into his daily regiment. Could he learn to speak to ambitions beyond the fiscal bottom line and touch the hearts of his team with something greater? Could he cultivate an environment where innovation stemmed not from fear of failure but from the courage to dare?

The sharp ring of his mobile phone tore through the room, halting his reverie. Alexander steadied his voice and picked up the device; it was an urgency that could not be ignored, another decision calling for his attention, his judgment. He responded in earnest, directing, clarifying, deciding. Yet beneath the facade of composure, Alexander knew the transformation he sought, the integration he yearned for, lingered just out of reach, shrouded in the mists of his hesitation.

Would he dare to brave those depths, to navigate that maze of introspection and self-renewal, to emerge not just as a leader of industry, but as a visionary capable of inspiring a legacy?

Unlock the CEO Within: A Realm of Revolutionary Leadership

Embarking on the journey from being a founder to stepping into the CEO role requires more than just a change in title. It demands a profound transformation in how you approach leadership, strategy, and personal development. This pivotal shift encompasses not only the mastering of practical tactics but also the embracing of mindset shifts that can elevate you from a driven founder to an impactful CEO. Through the integration of cutting-edge strategies, emotional intelligence, and advanced communication skills, you can unlock a level of leadership that propels both you and your business into new realms of success.

To lead with confidence, one must first understand that leadership is not just about making decisions but about fostering relationships, engaging teams, and driving vision forward with compassion and insight. This chapter delves deep into how to equip yourself with the essential tools to not only navigate the challenges of leadership but to thrive in them. By focusing on actionable strategies that refine your business acumen and personal development tools that elevate your self-awareness, you're provided with a holistic blueprint for transformation.

The cornerstone of impactful leadership lies in the ability to blend practical business strategies with personal growth. Engaging with your team, driving your business forward, and making a difference on a larger scale all start with the internal work of aligning your vision with your actions. Embracing emotional intelligence as a critical part of this journey allows for better decision-making, more meaningful relationships with your team, and a greater ability to navigate the complexities of leadership.

Moreover, advancing your communication skills is not just about conveying ideas but also about listening, understanding, and responding in ways that empower your team and foster a culture of transparency and innovation. This chapter guides you in leveraging these skills to not only improve your leadership abilities but also to enhance the performance and satisfaction of your team. Through dedicated practice and a commitment to continuous learning, you can transform the way you lead.

Adopting a holistic approach to CEO transformation is essential for those committed to making a significant impact. This means not only focusing on the business's bottom line but also understanding how leadership influences every aspect of the company. From strategic planning and marketing to business development and scaling, every element is tied back to how you lead. This chapter emphasizes the importance of integrating diverse knowledge and expertise to not only advance your own leadership capabilities but also to drive your business towards its full potential.

Every founder has the potential to become a revolutionary CEO, but it requires a driven mindset, a lifelong learner's approach, and an unwavering dedication to making a difference. By focusing on both actionable strategies and personal development, you're equipped with the necessary tools to navigate the complexities of leadership and drive your business forward without limits.

Remember, the journey from founder to CEO is not just about the destination but about the transformation along the way. By embracing these revolutionary strategies and dedicating yourself to continuous growth, you open the door to unlimited potential for yourself and your business. It's time to unlock the CEO within and lead with confidence.

Integrating Practical Tactics with Mindset Shifts

In today's fast-paced world, an effective leader is one who combines practical tactics with profound mindset shifts. It's like navigating a ship; you need both a strong rudder (mindset) and powerful sails (tactics) to ride the waves of change. Practical strategies might include clear goal-setting, data-driven decision-making, and efficient resource management. However, without the right mindset, these strategies can quickly become rudderless.

A leader's mindset operates as the foundation upon which all else builds. It encompasses emotional intelligence, a term that denotes the ability to understand and manage one's own emotions as well as the emotions of others. Emotional intelligence is crucial for leaders as it directly impacts team morale, motivation, and, ultimately, productivity. It's akin to knowing the sea's mood; you can't control the ocean, but understanding its rhythms can help you navigate more effectively.

Communication skills are another vital component of impactful leadership. Effective communication is not just about conveying information. It's about connecting with others, fostering mutual understanding, and motivating your team. A leader who communicates clearly and empathetically is like a captain who not only commands the ship but also listens to the crew, ensuring everyone is aligned and moving in the same direction.

Yet, integrating these components is not always straightforward. It requires a deliberate shift from focusing solely on external achievements to also cultivating internal growth. This evolution doesn't happen overnight but through continuous reflection, learning, and adaptation.

Effective leadership is a blend of tactical acumen, a growth-oriented mindset, emotional intelligence, and superior communication skills.

Equipping Yourself with Leadership Tools

To steer your business towards success, you must arm yourself with a diverse set of tools that bolster your leadership confidence and drive. Imagine a craftsman; their expertise is not solely dependent on their skill but also on the quality of their tools. Similarly, a leader's effectiveness is significantly enhanced by their toolkit, which should include strategic planning, decision-making capabilities, and an in-depth understanding of business analytics.

A core element of this toolkit is the ability to make informed decisions. In the realm of business, each decision can steer the company in new directions. Leaders must, therefore, be adept at analyzing data, weighing options, and foreseeing potential outcomes. It's a careful balance between intuition and logic, akin to a chef blending ingredients to create the perfect dish.

Equally important is the skill of strategic thinking. It involves not just envisioning the future but meticulously planning the steps to get there. This requires a deep understanding of the business landscape, including market trends, competitive dynamics, and customer preferences. Like a chess player, a strategic leader thinks several moves ahead, anticipating opponents' actions and preparing counter-strategies.

Moreover, confidence in leadership is not merely about self-assurance; it's about inspiring trust and respect in others. Confidence can be contagious, instilling a sense of security and motivation among team members. However, it must be rooted in competence and integrity, not arrogance or ignorance. This fine distinction is what separates truly great leaders from the merely assertive.

Yet, possessing these tools is not enough; leaders must constantly hone them. The business world is ever-evolving, and stagnation can lead to obsolescence. Thus, continuous learning and adaptation are essential. Leaders must remain students of their craft, always seeking new knowledge, insights, and perspectives.

How can you ensure that your leadership toolkit remains both versatile and effective in the face of constant change?

Holistic CEO Transformation through a Strategic Planning Framework

A comprehensive approach to CEO transformation necessitates blending actionable strategies with personal development tools. To effectively navigate this complex terrain, a Strategic Planning Framework can serve as a compass, guiding leaders through the intricacies of strategic development and execution.

Environmental Analysis

The first step in our framework is conducting an environmental analysis. This involves a thorough examination of both the external and internal landscapes to pinpoint opportunities and threats. Tools like SWOT (Strengths, Weaknesses, Opportunities, Threats) analysis, PESTEL (Political, Economic, Social, Technological, Environmental, Legal) analysis, and competitor analysis are invaluable here. Understanding the terrain is crucial—it's akin to a gardener assessing the soil and climate before planting.

Vision and Mission Development

Next, leaders must articulate a compelling vision and a clear mission for their company. This step is about setting a direction, much like a lighthouse, which provides guidance to ships in the dark. Exercises and templates can facilitate this process, helping leaders to crystallize their thoughts and communicate their vision and mission effectively.

Goal Setting

With a clear vision and mission, the next phase revolves around goal setting. Employing the SMART criteria ensures that goals are Specific, Measurable, Achievable, Relevant, and Time-bound. Additionally, the use of OKRs (Objectives and Key Results) can help in setting meaningful and achievable goals. This stage is about planting the seeds for future growth, ensuring that each goal aligns with the broader vision.

Strategy Formulation

Armed with set goals, leaders must then develop strategies to achieve them. This involves selecting the best route to reach the destination, like choosing the right path in a labyrinth. The framework provides guidance on different strategic approaches, such as differentiation, cost leadership, and focus, helping leaders to formulate effective strategies.

Implementation and Monitoring

Finally, the emphasis shifts to the effective execution and continuous monitoring of the strategic plan. Tools like Gantt charts, project management methodologies, and performance dashboards are instrumental in this phase. Just as a pilot must constantly adjust the plane's course, leaders must monitor progress and make necessary adjustments to ensure the strategy's successful implementation.

By breaking down the process into manageable components, this Strategic Planning Framework not only simplifies strategic development but also ensures that actionable strategies and personal development tools are seamlessly

integrated for holistic CEO transformation.

Incorporate Mindset Shifts with Practical Strategies for Lasting Transformation

Embracing a cutting-edge approach to leadership, the fusion of mindset shifts with practical strategies is the cornerstone of CEO evolution. By integrating emotional intelligence, communication skills, and innovative tactics, *CEOs equip themselves with a powerful toolkit for impactful leadership.* This visionary blend enables leaders to navigate challenges with resilience and finesse, fostering a culture of growth and adaptability within their organizations.

Putting It Into Practice: Transforming Your Leadership with Practical Strategies

It's crucial to integrate the practical strategies and mindset shifts discussed in this chapter. Use the following exercises and reflection prompts to guide you in your transformation and unlock your full potential as a leader.

1. **Conduct a self-assessment:**
   - Reflect on your current leadership style and identify areas for improvement.
   - Evaluate your emotional intelligence and communication skills.

- Determine which practical strategies you need to focus on to enhance your leadership effectiveness.

2. **Develop your strategic planning skills:**
- Familiarize yourself with the Strategic Planning Framework and its components.
- Practice conducting environmental analyses, such as SWOT, PESTEL, and competitor analysis.
- Engage in vision and mission development exercises to clarify your company's direction.

3. **Set SMART goals and implement OKRs:**
- Define specific, measurable, achievable, relevant, and time-bound goals for yourself and your organization.
- Introduce the concept of Objectives and Key Results (OKRs) to your team and align them with your company's vision and mission.
- Regularly review and adjust your goals and OKRs based on progress and changing circumstances.

4. **Enhance your decision-making capabilities:**
- Practice data-driven decision-making by analyzing relevant metrics and insights.
- Develop a process for weighing options, considering potential outcomes, and making informed decisions.
- Seek input from your team and stakeholders to gain diverse perspectives and make more inclusive decisions.

5. **Cultivate your emotional intelligence:**
- Practice self-awareness by regularly reflecting on your emotions, strengths, and weaknesses.
- Develop empathy by actively listening to your team members and considering their perspectives.
- Work on managing your emotions and responding constructively to challenging situations.

6. **Improve your communication skills:**
- Practice active listening and seek to understand others' viewpoints before responding.
- Develop your ability to articulate your vision, goals, and expectations clearly and persuasively.
- Provide regular feedback to your team and create opportunities for open dialogue and collaboration.

7. **Embrace continuous learning and adaptation:**
- Stay informed about industry trends, market developments, and emerging technologies.
- Seek out learning opportunities, such as workshops, conferences, and mentoring relationships.
- Foster a culture of continuous improvement and encourage your team to embrace learning and growth.

Remember, transforming your leadership is an ongoing process that requires dedication, self-reflection, and a willingness to adapt. By consistently applying these practical strategies and embracing the necessary mindset shifts, you'll be well on your way to becoming the visionary CEO your organization needs.

Start by assessing your current leadership style and identifying areas for improvement. Then, focus on developing your strategic planning skills, setting SMART goals, and enhancing your decision-making capabilities. As you progress, prioritize cultivating your emotional intelligence and improving your communication skills to foster a more engaging and collaborative work environment.

By putting these strategies into practice and committing to continuous learning and growth, you'll unlock your full potential as a leader and drive your organization towards unprecedented success. Embrace the journey of transformation and watch as your leadership skills flourish, enabling you to navigate challenges with confidence and grace.

Chapter 5

Cultivating a Growth Mindset

Gray clouds whispered threats of a storm as Julian stood, arms crossed, at the edge of the building site. His company had just lost its biggest contract, and the skeleton of unfinished steel mocked him with the echo of what might have been. Julian recalled the long journey that had brought him to this precipice, the ascension from middle management to CEO, a position once gilded and now tarnished with the specter of failure.

He watched a crow navigate the gusting wind, its wings adjusting deftly to unseen currents. This, too, was a skill he needed – not just to right himself in turbulent skies but to use the tempest itself as an advantage. The path forward was not a return to the forgotten order but an embrace of the chaos that now reigned. Julian had learned from bitter experience that missteps were teachers garbed in shadow, their lessons harsh but invaluable in etching expertise and resilience across one's character.

Julian's soles rhythmically crunched on the gravel as he navigated through the debris of the worksite, each step a beating in the heart of a silent world of concrete and steel. He paused to watch workers dismantle a partly erected wall. The clangs of hammer on metal were a clarion call to reforge and reshape not just the mismanaged project but his leadership philosophy. It was time for innovation, time to foster the adaptability and creativity simmering beneath the surface of his team. Failure was but a prelude to ingenuity.

Inside his stark office, maps and charts lay spread like war plans, campaigns that had seen better days. Here, seated at the head of a long, barren table, the familiar musk of ambition and forethought hung in the air. It was in this very room that the ideas and strategies of yesteryear had been borne – but the ashes of the past held no sway in the emerging narrative of his leadership. Julian wondered, not for the first time, if the strategies of old were the shackles that bound his company to obsolescence.

As the windows rattled with the first drops of rain, he acknowledged that resilience was not a fortress to shield from the change but a vessel to navigate through it. Each droplet resonated with the reality that continuous improvement was a cycle of response, of growth, of personal evolution. Julian knew his next steps would chart a course through untested waters – where the vision of a CEO was measured not by the steadiness of their hand but by their ability to dance with the unknown. And wasn't the essence of life itself a dance with chaos, a perpetual motion between form and void?

In the dimming light, as shadows crept across the room, a thought lingered in Julian's mind, reflective and pervasive. How does one measure the distance between the CEO of the past and the leader the future demands?

The Journey From Resilience to Revolution

CEOs and founders stepping into the entrepreneurial limelight often find themselves at a crossroads between maintaining the status quo and venturing into the unknown to revolutionize their sectors. **Cultivating a growth mindset** is not merely a nice-to-have; it's a necessity for those committed to transforming from a founder into a CEO capable of scaling their company beyond limits. It embodies the essence of embracing challenges, learning from failures, and relentlessly pursuing opportunities for growth. By integrating a growth-centric perspective into their leadership arsenal, CEOs position themselves and their organizations on a trajectory toward groundbreaking innovation and unparalleled success.

Embracing challenges is the first step in this transformative journey. It's about more than just acknowledging difficulties; it's about **seeing them as opportunities** to refine strategies, enhance decision-making, and strengthen resilience. This chapter delves into real-world strategies for converting obstacles into stepping stones, demonstrating how a shift in mindset from avoidance to engagement can lay the foundation for breakthrough achievements in business development and leadership.

Failure, as much as it is dreaded, is an unparalleled teacher. A growth mindset reframes failure not as a symbol of defeat but as a catalyst for learning and progression. It's about extracting valuable lessons from every setback and using them to forge ahead with even greater determination. This segment reveals how successful CEOs treat failures as critical learning moments, providing actionable insights on fostering an organizational culture that encourages experimentation, embraces calculated risks, and turns temporary setbacks into essential growth opportunities.

Continuously seeking opportunities for improvement signifies a leader's commitment to never settling. It spells the difference between good and great, between stagnation and scaling. This chapter highlights the significance of being a *lifelong learner*, constantly pursuing advanced education and expanding one's expertise across diverse domains. It outlines practical tips for staying ahead of industry trends, engaging with cutting-edge research, and applying new knowledge to drive innovative solutions that address the needs of underserved communities effectively.

Resilience is the linchpin of a growth mindset. It's what enables CEOs to ride the relentless waves of business uncertainties without losing sight of their vision. This section shows you how to develop an unshakeable core of resilience, ensuring you can weather storms, adapt strategies on the fly, and keep your team focused and motivated through periods of change or challenge.

Innovation within an organization doesn't happen in a vacuum; it's driven by leaders who see beyond the horizon. Here, you'll discover how adopting a growth mindset propels not just personal development but also catalyzes organizational transformation. By fostering an environment that values continuous learning, adaptability, and the pursuit of excellence, you empower your team to contribute ideas that can scale the company and make a lasting impact.

Lastly, embracing change is foundational to any growth-oriented journey. It's about more than flexibility; it's a willingness to dismantle and rebuild, even when the path of least resistance suggests minor adjustments. This part of the chapter imparts strategies for fostering adaptability in your approach to leadership and business development, making it clear that the cultivation of a growth mindset is an ongoing, dynamic process that requires commitment, courage, and a relentless drive to make a difference.

By weaving these elements together, CEOs can liberate themselves from the constraints of conventional thinking, opening doors to unimaginable possibilities. As you integrate these practices into your leadership repertoire, you not only transform your business; you reinvent yourself, showcasing what it truly means to evolve from a founder to a visionary CEO.

Embrace Challenges, Learn from Failures, and Actively Seek Opportunities for Growth

Imagine you're navigating a complex maze. Each wrong turn you take doesn't spell the end of your journey; rather, it exposes paths you hadn't considered before. This analogy mirrors the entrepreneurial path where failures are not dead-ends but detours, leading to unexpected insights and opportunities. It's through these missteps that CEOs learn the most crucial lessons about their business, their team, and themselves.

Furthermore, actively seeking opportunities for growth requires a ceaseless curiosity and willingness to step out of comfort zones. It involves challenging the status quo, experimenting with new strategies, and being open to feedback and change. This proactive approach not only accelerates personal development but also fosters a culture of continuous improvement within the organization.

Learning from failures, meanwhile, instills a sense of humility and perspective. It's a clear reminder that there's always room for improvement, regardless of past successes. This humility, when fused with the determination to learn and grow, creates a powerful catalyst for personal and professional transformation.

Learning to embrace challenges, learn from failures, and actively seek growth opportunities is paramount for CEOs committed to evolving and driving their organizations forward.

Develop Resilience, Continuously Improve Your Skills, and Drive Innovation Within Your Organization

Resilience is not merely about bouncing back from setbacks; it's about emerging stronger and more determined. For CEOs, developing resilience is essential for navigating the unpredictable waters of the business world. It requires a steadfast commitment to personal and professional growth, even in the face of adversity. Just as a tree bends in a strong wind but doesn't break, resilient leaders adapt, learn, and continue to move forward.

Continuous improvement of skills is a lifelong journey. In the rapidly changing business landscape, staying ahead means being a perpetual student. Leaders must be dedicated to honing their expertise and embracing new knowledge. This commitment to learning not only enhances personal capabilities but also inspires those around them to elevate their own skills, creating a ripple effect of improvement across the entire organization.

Driving innovation requires a blend of audacity and creativity. It's about seeing beyond the present, imagining what could be, and daring to make those visions a reality. Innovation isn't just about introducing new products or services; it's about thinking differently, challenging existing processes, and finding more efficient ways to solve problems. Leaders who prioritize innovation not only secure a competitive edge for their businesses but also contribute to a culture that values curiosity and out-of-the-box thinking.

Consider a forest where diverse species thrive together, each contributing to the ecosystem in unique ways. Similarly, an innovative organization values the diverse perspectives and skills of its members, understanding that breakthrough ideas often come from the most unexpected places. This synergy not only fuels creativity but also strengthens the organization's resilience in the face of challenges.

Building Resilience: A Practical Framework for CEOs and Their Teams

Resilience is not an innate trait but a skill that can be developed and strengthened over time. As a CEO, it's crucial to not only cultivate your own resilience but also foster it within your team. Here's a practical framework to help you build resilience both personally and organizationally:

1. **Develop a growth mindset:** Embrace challenges as opportunities for growth and learning. Encourage your team to view setbacks as temporary and as a chance to improve

and innovate.

2. **Practice self-awareness**: Regularly reflect on your thoughts, emotions, and reactions to stress. Recognize your strengths and areas for improvement, and work on developing emotional intelligence.

3. **Establish a support network**: Build strong relationships with mentors, peers, and trusted advisors who can provide guidance, support, and honest feedback. Encourage your team to do the same and foster a culture of open communication and collaboration.

4. **Prioritize self-care:** Take care of your physical, mental, and emotional well-being. Engage in regular exercise, practice mindfulness, and prioritize work-life balance. Encourage your team to do the same and lead by example.

5. **Cultivate adaptability:** Develop flexibility in your thinking and approach to problem-solving. Encourage your team to embrace change and be open to new ideas and strategies.

6. **Learn from failures:** Treat failures as valuable learning experiences. Conduct post-mortem analyses to identify lessons learned and areas for improvement. Share these insights with your team and encourage a culture of continuous learning.

7. **Celebrate successes:** Acknowledge and celebrate both individual and team accomplishments. Recognizing progress and achievements helps build confidence and motivation, which are essential components of resilience.

8. **Foster a resilient organizational culture**: Create a culture that values perseverance, adaptability, and continuous learning. Encourage open communication, support risk-taking, and provide resources for employee development and well-being.

By implementing this framework, you'll not only enhance your own resilience as a leader but also create a team and organization that can withstand challenges, adapt to change, and thrive in the face of adversity.

Foster Adaptability and a Willingness to Embrace Change for Personal and Professional Development

In an ever-evolving world, adaptability is not just an advantage; it's a necessity. The ability to pivot in response to new challenges and opportunities is a hallmark of successful leaders. Embracing change doesn't mean haphazardly shifting directions; it involves thoughtful evaluation and strategic realignment to ensure the company remains on a path to success.

Adaptability can be likened to water – it's fluid, flexible, and finds its way around obstacles. Just as water shapes itself into the container it's in but retains its essence, adaptable leaders adjust their strategies and approaches without losing sight of their core values and visions. This fluidity enables them to navigate uncertainties with grace and make informed decisions that propel their organizations forward.

The willingness to embrace change also opens doors to personal growth. It frees leaders from the constraints of their comfort zones and empowers them to explore new territories, both in their individual capabilities and within their industries. This exploration is not without risk, but it's through these ventures into the unknown that profound learning and development occur.

Combining adaptability with a growth mindset transforms challenges into stepping stones, where each step, regardless of its immediate outcome, contributes to personal and professional development. This approach not only accelerates a leader's evolution but also establishes a resilient, innovative, and forward-looking organizational culture.

By fostering adaptability, cultivating resilience, and relentlessly pursuing growth and innovation, leaders can navigate the complexities of their roles with confidence and drive transformative changes within their organizations.

Embracing challenges, learning from failures, and actively seeking opportunities for growth are not just principles but guiding lights for CEOs in their evolution. **By committing to a growth mindset, CEOs lay the foundation for continuous improvement and innovation within their organizations.** Through resilience and a thirst for knowledge, they pave the way for revolutionary breakthroughs and cutting-edge strategies. **Driving change within themselves and their teams, CEOs empower their organizations to scale, engage with diverse perspectives, and make a difference in underserved communities.** *This dedication to personal and professional growth is not only admirable but essential in today's fast-paced business landscape.* As leaders, it is imperative to remain committed to honing skills, fostering adaptability, and embracing change, as these are the cornerstones of success.

Putting It Into Practice: Cultivating Your Growth Mindset

Now that you understand the importance of a growth mindset and its role in your evolution as a CEO, it's time to put these concepts into action. Use the following exercises and reflection prompts to cultivate your own growth mindset and foster it within your organization:

1. **Reframe challenges:**
   - Identify a current challenge you're facing as a CEO.
   - Reframe this challenge as an opportunity for growth and learning.
   - Develop a plan to tackle the challenge with a focus on the lessons you can learn from the experience.

2. **Learn from failures:**
   - Reflect on a recent failure or setback you've experienced.
   - Analyze the situation to identify the lessons learned and areas for improvement.
   - Share these insights with your team and discuss how you can apply them to future projects or decisions.

3. **Seek growth opportunities:**
   - Identify areas where you want to improve your skills or knowledge as a CEO.
   - Research resources, such as books, workshops, or mentors,

can help you grow in these areas.

- Commit to a specific learning goal and create a plan to achieve it.

4. **Practice self-reflection:**

- Set aside time each day or week for self-reflection.
- Use this time to assess your thoughts, emotions, and reactions to challenges and successes.
- Identify patterns or areas for improvement and develop strategies to address them.

5. **Foster a growth mindset culture:**

- Communicate the importance of a growth mindset to your team.
- Encourage experimentation, risk-taking, and learning from failures.
- Celebrate team members who demonstrate a growth mindset and share the lessons they have learned with others.

6. **Build resilience:**

- Implement the practical framework for building resilience from the previous section.
- Regularly assess your progress and make adjustments as needed.
- Encourage your team to adopt resilience-building practices and provide support and resources to help them do so.

7. **Embrace change:**

- Identify an area where you or your organization have been resistant to change.

- Develop a plan to embrace change in this area, focusing on the potential benefits and opportunities it presents.

- Communicate this plan to your team and involve them in the process of implementing the change.

Remember, cultivating a growth mindset is an ongoing process that requires commitment and consistent effort. By regularly engaging in these practices and leading by example, you'll not only transform your own mindset but also inspire your team to embrace challenges, learn from failures, and continuously seek opportunities for growth. As you progress on this journey, you'll develop the resilience, adaptability, and innovative thinking needed to scale your company and make a lasting impact as a visionary CEO.

Chapter 6

The Art of Effective

Communication

Beneath the half-shuttered glow of an early evening sun, Priscilla stood silent in the wide expanse of her office, a tableau of the city sprawling before her. The glow slipped through blinds and slanted across her desk, casting long shadows across the pages of reports and charts—an impressive view from the 50th floor made unhappy by her contemplation.

The room hummed with tranquility found in the last hours of a workday when the bustle of keystrokes and the murmur of voices had ebbed, leaving the echo of his thoughts more audible. Priscilla, the CEO, whose days were often besieged by decisions, found herself grappling with a void that could not be filled by conventional prowess alone.

Today, hierwar was with communication—or the lack thereof. Priscilla pondered, among the pillars of data and strategy, about the voices not heard, the sentiments not shared. Her fingers brushed against an open email, a simple enough request on the surface, but underneath, it carried the weight of relationships frayed by poor communication. The challenge was not in the fiscal reports but in the hearts and minds of those who compiled them. How had she not foreseen the chasm that had grown in her team?

A colleague once told her that the soil of trust must be fertile before the seeds of collaboration can grow. Those words now wrestled in her mind with every report that whispered of discontent. She walked to the vast window, where the city lights began their nightly chorus, and she longed for that melody of mutual understanding in her own office.

A soft knock broke his reverie, and Marc, her analyst, slipped into the room with the grace of one used to cushion the day's rough edges. "Anything before I head out, Priscilla?" he asked, the dusk painting him in the silhouette of efficiency. There was something in his steady gaze that compelled her to share, to reach across the invisible divide of titles and positions.

Priscilla did not answer at once but instead focused on the reflection of their two figures, side by side yet worlds apart. She turned and spoke, not as a CEO to his analyst, but as a fellow traveler on the road of uncertainty, "I'm thinking about how to really listen, Marc. To hear the worries, the hopes. . . the unspoken. How do we ensure that every voice is valued here?"

He considered her, weighing his words like coins of a precious metal. "It starts by asking that question and wanting to hear the answer, I think," he said, the soft sound of his departing steps signaling the day's close.

Alone once more, Priscilla faced the windows and the gathering night. There, in the space where light danced with shadow, she resolved to bridge the gap of unspoken words with actions. Tomorrow, she would call a meeting—not to dictate but to invite dialogue, to foster the openness that had become so elusive.

As Priscilla switched off the lights and the room surrendered to twilight, she mulled over the path ahead. Would the courage to be vulnerable, to lead not by word but by example, reveal itself as strong enough to change the fabric of her team? Would the transformation begin with unspoken acknowledgements becoming spoken truths?

She left the office, her mind cultivating plans like stars ready to break the night's depth. Could transparency and empathy light the firmament of his company's future?

Mastering the Language of Leadership

At the heart of transformative leadership lies the power of effective communication. It's a tool that far too often goes underutilized, yet its impact on leadership and organizational success cannot be overstated. This dedicated exploration into the art of communication reveals that the journey from founder to CEO requires more than just a great business idea or breakthrough innovation—it demands a commitment to developing strong relationships, fostering open dialogue, and providing clear direction to your team. In essence, **effective communication** is the lifeblood of successful leadership and a pivotal step in transforming your business.

The transition from a hands-on founder to a visionary CEO involves scaling not just the physical aspects of your company but also the quality of its internal dialogue. **Building strong relationships** and fostering open dialogue are foundational to this process. They empower teams, engage stakeholders, and create an environment where innovative ideas flourish. Here, being a committed listener is as critical as being an articulate speaker. It demands a revolutionary approach to daily interactions, one where every conversation is an opportunity to reinforce trust and collaboration.

Providing **clear direction** is another cornerstone of effective communication. It's about stripping away the ambiguity that can cloud your team's vision, leaving them empowered with the clarity and confidence to move forward. This doesn't just happen. It requires a CEO to be deeply committed to transparency and to possess an unwavering determination to convey the company's mission, goals, and expectations with precision. This clarity becomes the compass that guides your team through the challenges of scaling and innovation.

Creating a **culture of trust, collaboration, and accountability** within your team is crucial. It transforms workplaces into communities where commitment to the collective goal drives performance. This culture nurtures the spirit of innovation, encourages taking responsible risks, and acknowledges efforts, making a significant impact on your company's ability to scale and tackle underserved markets effectively. As you impart this culture through your communication, you lay the groundwork for a resilient, adaptable organization.

Effective communication also aligns **team members toward common goals** by prioritizing transparent and empathetic dialogue. It's about connecting on a human level, ensuring that every team member not only understands the 'what' and the 'why' behind their tasks but also feels valued and understood. This level of empathy in communication fosters a shared sense of purpose, driving your team to achieve breakthrough performance and innovative solutions that could redefine markets.

Empowerment through effective communication is not just a strategy. It's a manifestation of your leadership ethos. It's about being a lifelong learner, open to the nuances of human interaction, and committed to refining your message until it resonates with your audience—your team. By honing this skill, you position yourself not just as a CEO but as a leader, making a difference and scaling not only your company but also the impact you have on your team, your stakeholders, and the communities you serve.

Through the lens of communication, we see that the path from founder to CEO is intrinsically linked to how well one can engage, inspire, and align their team with the company's vision. This chapter, therefore, isn't just about communicating effectively; it's about transforming your intent into action, your vision into reality, and your words into the foundation upon which your company's culture is built. Embrace these principles, and you'll have taken a significant step in transforming your business and yourself.

Building strong relationships and fostering open dialogue through effective communication are the bedrocks upon which transformative leadership is built. Just as the roots of a tree intertwine with the soil to provide stability and nourishment, effective communication also serves to anchor and nurture the relationships within a team. It's this interconnectedness that enables the tree to weather storms and thrive, a metaphor that underscores the importance of strong communication in creating resilient teams.

In the business landscape, communication isn't just about the exchange of information. It's about creating an environment where every voice is heard and every concern is addressed. This democratization of dialogue fosters a culture where trust flourishes. When a leader actively listens and engages with their team on a deeper level, it signals that every opinion is valued. This not only empowers individuals but also cultivates a sense of belonging.

However, achieving open dialogue isn't without its challenges. It requires a committed effort to break down the hierarchies that often silence voices. Think of a garden where every plant, regardless of its kind, is given equal access to sunlight, water, and nutrients. Just as these resources enable each plant to contribute its best to the ecosystem, so does an inclusive communication strategy that allows every team member to bring their strengths to the table.

The role of a leader is pivotal in nurturing this ecosystem. It starts with embodying the change one wishes to see. Leading by example, acknowledging one's own vulnerabilities, and encouraging transparency can revolutionize the dynamics of team interaction. It shifts the narrative from one of competition to collaboration, where mistakes are viewed as opportunities for growth rather than reasons for castigation.

Effective communication is the cornerstone of strong relationships and open dialogue.

Providing clear direction and creating a culture of trust, collaboration, and accountability within your team is akin to navigating a ship through tumultuous seas. A captain who communicates the route clearly trusts his crew's abilities and holds them accountable for their tasks will not only navigate the storm but also strengthen the team's unity and resilience. This analogy illustrates the fundamental role of effective leadership communication in steering the team towards success.

Clarity of direction ensures that everyone on the team is aligned with the organizational goals. It involves articulating the vision, mission, and objectives so distinctly that each member understands their role in the grand scheme. Imagine a puzzle where each piece has a unique place. Without understanding the bigger picture, it's challenging for team members to see where their pieces fit. Clear communication from the leadership acts as the puzzle's box cover, guiding each member to place their piece correctly.

Trust is the fabric that holds successful teams together. It's built on the premise that leaders will be transparent in their directions and intentions. Leaders demonstrating trust in their team's abilities empower them to take ownership of their tasks. This empowered environment encourages innovation, as team members feel safe to explore new ideas without fear of retribution for mistakes.

Collaboration and accountability are the natural outcomes of a culture rooted in trust and clear direction. When teams work collaboratively, pooling their skills and resources, they achieve more than what could be achieved individually. However, collaboration shouldn't mean the absence of accountability. On the contrary, when team members are held accountable for their contributions, it reinforces the importance of their role and encourages them to take responsibility seriously.

But how can leaders ensure they're navigating their team toward a culture of trust, collaboration, and accountability?

Aligning team members towards common goals by prioritizing transparent and empathetic communication can be thought of as conducting an orchestra. Each member plays a different instrument, contributing unique sounds, but when directed with skill and understanding, they create harmonious music. Similarly, in a team, diverse skills and perspectives can achieve remarkable results when guided by transparent and empathetic leadership.

Transparency in communication involves sharing the necessary information and the rationale behind decisions. It's about letting the light in, ensuring there are no hidden agendas that can sow seeds of doubt among team members. Transparent leadership is open, honest, and forthcoming, which engenders trust and respect.

Empathy, on the other hand, ensures that this transparency is delivered with understanding and care. It requires leaders to step into their team members' shoes to understand their perspectives, concerns, and motivations. By prioritizing empathetic communication, leaders demonstrate that their decisions are made with the team's wellbeing in mind, fostering a supportive and cohesive environment.

Developing Empathetic Listening Skills: A Practical Framework

Empathetic listening is a critical component of effective communication and a key skill for transformative leaders. It involves not just hearing the words spoken but also understanding the emotions, concerns, and perspectives behind them. Here's a practical framework to help you develop and cultivate empathetic listening skills in your workplace:

1. **Practice active listening:** Give your full attention to the speaker, avoid interruptions, and minimize distractions. Use non-verbal cues like nodding and maintaining eye contact to show your engagement.

2. **Suspend judgment:** Approach each conversation with an open mind, setting aside your own biases and preconceptions. Focus on understanding the speaker's perspective before forming your own opinions.

3. **Ask clarifying questions:** Engage in the conversation by asking questions that help you better understand the speaker's viewpoint. This shows your interest and helps you gain a deeper understanding of their thoughts and feelings.

4. **Reflect and paraphrase:** Summarize what you've heard in your own words to ensure you've understood the speaker correctly. This also demonstrates that you're actively listening and engaging with their message.

5. **Validate emotions**: Acknowledge and validate the speaker's feelings, even if you don't necessarily agree with their perspective. This creates a safe space for open and honest dialogue.

6. **Offer support:** Show your understanding and offer support where appropriate. This could include providing resources, offering guidance, or simply expressing your empathy and willingness to help.

7. **Follow up:** After the conversation, follow up on any action items or commitments made. This demonstrates your sincerity and helps build trust and accountability.

By incorporating these steps into your daily interactions, you'll foster a culture of empathetic listening that strengthens relationships, promotes understanding, and drives collaboration within your team.

Linking transparency and empathy in communication does not happen overnight. It's a skill honed over time and with dedicated effort. But the rewards are manifold—teams that trust their leaders and feel understood are more committed, passionate, and aligned with organizational goals. They are teams that not only meet targets but exceed them, transforming challenges into opportunities for growth.

By building relationships based on open dialogue, providing clear direction rooted in trust, and aligning team members through transparent and empathetic communication, leaders can create an unstoppable force towards achieving their vision.

Effective communication lies at the core of successful CEO leadership. As we journeyed through this chapter, we unveiled the essential components that define this art. **Building strong relationships, fostering open dialogue, and providing clear direction** are not just strategies; they are the pillars that uphold a thriving organizational culture. By embracing these principles, CEOs can sculpt a work environment steeped in **trust, collaboration, and accountability**.

Guided by the compass of **transparent and empathetic communication**, leaders propel their teams towards a shared vision. By aligning every member towards common objectives, the organization gains momentum and strength like never before. The ability to convey ideas clearly, listen intently, and inspire action becomes a **revolutionary tool for transformative leadership**.

So, as you reflect on the significance of effective

communication in your role, remember that it isn't just about words exchanged but about the impact those words create. Your commitment to honing these skills will not only elevate your leadership but also ripple through your team, inspiring a culture of passion, innovation, and unwavering dedication.

Putting It Into Practice: Mastering Effective Communication

Now that you understand the importance of effective communication and its role in your journey from founder to CEO, it's time to put these principles into action. Use the following exercises and reflection prompts to cultivate your communication skills and foster a culture of open dialogue, trust, and collaboration within your organization:

1. **Assess your communication style:**

- Reflect on your current communication habits and identify areas for improvement.

- Seek feedback from your team members on how you can communicate more effectively.

- Identify any barriers to open communication within your team and brainstorm solutions.

2. **Practice active listening:**

- In your next team meeting, focus on actively listening to each speaker without interruption.

- Use non-verbal cues to show your engagement and ask clarifying questions to ensure understanding.

- Reflect on how active listening impacts the quality and outcome of the meeting.

3. **Foster open dialogue:**

- Create regular opportunities for your team members to share their thoughts, ideas, and concerns.

- Encourage participation from all team members and create a safe space for diverse perspectives.

- Model vulnerability by sharing your own challenges and learnings as a leader.

4. **Provide clear direction:**

- Develop a clear and concise communication plan for your team, outlining goals, expectations, and responsibilities.

- Ensure that each team member understands their role and how it contributes to the overall vision.

- Regularly review and update your communication plan based on feedback and changing needs.

5. **Build trust and accountability:**

- Follow through on your commitments and hold yourself and

your team accountable for their actions.

- Celebrate successes and learn from failures as a team, fostering a culture of growth and collaboration.

- Regularly recognize and appreciate the contributions of your team members.

6. **Practice empathetic communication:**

- In your interactions with team members, focus on understanding their perspectives and emotions.

- Use the practical framework for empathetic listening to guide your conversations.

- Reflect on how empathetic communication impacts your relationships and the overall team dynamic.

7. **Continuously refine your skills:**

- Seek out opportunities for learning and growth, such as communication workshops or leadership seminars.

- Regularly assess your progress and set new goals for improving your communication skills.

- Encourage your team members also to prioritize their communication skills and provide resources for their development.

By consistently applying these practices and making

effective communication a priority, you'll not only enhance your own leadership skills but also foster a culture of trust, collaboration, and growth within your organization. Remember, mastering effective communication is an ongoing journey that requires commitment, self-reflection, and a willingness to adapt and improve. Embrace the process, and watch as your words become the catalyst for transformative change within your team and your business.

Chapter 7

Delegation and Empowerment in Leadership

In the half-light of the early morning, James Barclay stood alone in the corner of the expansive yet stark office, its walls lined with charts and graphs that screamed of data and deadlines. A cup of coffee, still full, had gone cold on his desk. He stared through the window, his gaze piercing the looming cityscape. He was the CEO, but the office felt less like a boardroom and more like a battleground where trust and control fought a silent war.

James had always been a solitary figure at the helm of his team. He had led with precision, his hands steering every decision, every project. But the weight of carrying every detail had finally sunk into his shoulders like lead, bending him into a bow of exhaustion. A team of bright minds surrounded him, yet he had held the reins so tightly that their lights had dimmed.

He remembered the faces of his staff in yesterday's meeting; they were there but not present. Emily had ideas sparkling in her eyes, but they never reached her lips. Mark had shuffled his feet, his expertise untapped, locked behind a dampened spirit. This was not the team he had dreamt of building.

His mind wandered to an old mentor's words, spoken in the autumn of his youth, "Empowerment, James, is the catalyst of leadership. "

Those words rustled through his mind like a leaf in the wind, and he realized the problem was him. He had to change the course, to let go and allow each member to claim their space, their responsibility, and their power to make decisions. Could he put trust in others to share the burden of leadership?

A shaft of sunlight broke through the city's monoliths, casting a golden beam across the room that settled on a framed photo of the team, brighter now in the new light. He saw potential, his and theirs together, a shared horizon.

As the office began to stir with the arrival of his team, he made a silent vow. Today, he would start the change. Today, he would ask Emily for her thoughts on the new project and encourage Mark to lead the brainstorming session. He'd distribute tasks that aligned with each person's strengths, not a random assignment of duties to be checked off a list.

The aroma of fresh coffee drifted from the kitchen, breaking his reverie, as Rebecca, who led client relations, offered a warm mug, her smile tentative but hopeful. He took a grateful sip, the richness reviving something within. Perhaps the warmth he felt was not from the coffee but from the spark of a new beginning that promised growth not only for the business but for every soul within these walls.

In the clarity of this newfound resolve, James questioned whether he truly understood the power of letting go. Could he learn to trust not just in his ability but in the creativity and drive of his team? Would their potential truly soar if he stepped back and allowed autonomy to lead the way?

Unleashing the Power of Your Team

In today's fast-paced and competitive landscape, the ability to lead effectively is more crucial than ever. A cornerstone of successful leadership lies in the art of delegation and empowerment. Trusting your team members and empowering them to take ownership of their responsibilities is not just a leadership strategy; it's a breakthrough approach to driving innovation and scaling your company. This insightful exploration delves into why every founder transitioning into a CEO role must master the delicate balance of delegating tasks while fostering a culture of empowerment and autonomy within their teams.

Delegation and empowerment are more than just buzzwords; they are the engines of growth and productivity in the modern business world. To truly maximize your team's potential, a CEO needs to strategize the distribution of tasks effectively. This doesn't simply mean assigning tasks; it involves identifying the strengths of each team member and aligning these strengths with the organization's objectives. It's about making a difference in how work is approached and executed, setting the stage for breakthrough performance and revolutionary outcomes.

Trusting your team members and empowering them requires not only a leap of faith but also a committed effort to develop and nurture individual capabilities. A driven founder knows that for a team to be fully engaged and maximally productive, each member needs to feel a sense of ownership over their work. By granting your team autonomy, you signal trust and respect for their skills and decisions, paving the way for a dynamic and innovative work environment.

Fostering **a sense of autonomy** among team members isn't about taking a hands-off approach; it's about being strategically hands-on. It involves providing the right tools, resources, and support they need to perform their tasks independently. This strategic distribution of tasks elevates the collective capability of the team, making the delegation process not just effective but transformative. It transforms the workflow into a more efficient, productive, and engaging system, contributing significantly to the scalability and sustainability of the business.

Leveraging delegation to **maximize team potential**

involves a deep understanding of each team member's unique skills and how these can be harnessed for the greater good of the organization. Engaging team members in roles that challenge and excite them promotes a culture of continuous learning and growth. This not only empowers the team but also ensures that the company remains at the cutting-edge, ready to adapt to changes and seize opportunities.

By empowering your team through strategic delegation, you're not only optimizing operational efficiency; you're also *creating leaders within your organization* who are committed to driving the company forward.

Trust Your Team Members and Empower Them

Trusting your team members and empowering them to take ownership of their responsibilities is akin to giving someone the key to a treasure chest rather than just showing them where it is hidden. It's not just about belief in their abilities; it's about actively handing over control, allowing them to unlock and explore their potential to the fullest. This act of faith can transform a group of individuals into a cohesive, driven unit capable of achieving far more than what's possible through individual effort alone.

Trust plays a pivotal role here. It's the foundation upon which empowerment is built. Trusting someone with a task indicates that you believe in their capability to handle it, but empowerment goes a step further. It equips them with the authority and autonomy to make decisions regarding the task. This means stepping back to let them navigate the path forward, make mistakes, learn, and, ultimately, grow.

Imagine you're teaching someone to ride a bike. Initially, you might hold onto the back to keep them steady. But real learning only begins when you let go. They might wobble, even fall, but that's where the real growth happens. Just as a cyclist gains balance through practice and falls, employees develop confidence and competence when they're entrusted with autonomy and the opportunity to own their responsibilities.

Empowerment also involves providing the resources, support, and guidance they need to succeed. It's about creating an environment where failure is seen not as a setback but as a stepping stone to growth and learning. This approach fosters innovation, as team members feel more comfortable taking calculated risks and exploring new ideas when they know their leader trusts them to navigate through the resulting outcomes.

To truly empower your team, regular feedback and open communication are essential. It helps in adjusting courses, celebrating successes, and addressing challenges collaboratively. Moreover, empowerment is not a one-time task but a continuous process. It requires constant nurturing, patience, and a commitment to developing capabilities within your team over time.

The key to unlocking the vast potential within your team lies in trusting and empowering them to take ownership.

Fostering Autonomy and Strategic Distribution

Fostering a sense of autonomy and strategic distribution of tasks among team members is paramount for effective delegation. It's not just about assigning tasks; it's about matching responsibilities with individual strengths and interests to maximize engagement and productivity. When team members feel that their roles are tailored to their capabilities and aspirations, their investment in the success of the project increases significantly.

Creating a framework where autonomy is valued requires a deliberate shift from micromanagement to macro-management. Leaders must resist the urge to control every detail, opting instead to set clear expectations, provide the necessary resources, and then step back. This approach allows employees to explore their roles fully, apply their creativity, and take the initiative, confident in the knowledge that they have their leader's support.

Think of it as gardening. A gardener doesn't grow plants; they create the conditions under which plants can grow. Similarly, leaders don't directly execute every task. Instead, they nurture an environment where team members can flourish in their roles. By strategically distributing tasks and fostering autonomy, leaders can ensure that every part of the garden gets the attention it needs to thrive.

But autonomy doesn't mean isolation. Regular check-ins, feedback, and support are crucial for maintaining alignment with organizational goals and ensuring that autonomy doesn't turn into abdication. This balance fosters a culture of responsibility, where each team member feels accountable not just for their tasks but for the success of the team and the organization as a whole.

Effective delegation involves recognizing the unique contributions each team member can make. It's about understanding their strengths, weaknesses, and motivational drivers. When tasks are aligned with individual skills and interests, the quality of work and level of engagement improve dramatically. It's a strategy that not only boosts productivity but also fosters professional growth and satisfaction among team members.

What if creating an environment of autonomy could be the key to unlocking unprecedented levels of creativity and efficiency in your organization?

Maximize Team Potential Through Delegation

Maximizing team potential and driving productivity through delegation is not just about assigning tasks; it's about empowering your team. It requires a thoughtful approach where the strengths and interests of team members are aligned with the organization's goals to create a synergy that propels the business forward. This process not only enhances efficiency but also nurtures a culture of ownership and innovation among team members.

When delegation is done right, it becomes a powerful tool for development. Team members are exposed to new challenges and opportunities that stretch their capabilities, encouraging learning and growth. This developmental aspect of delegation is crucial for building a resilient and adaptable workforce ready to take on the ever-evolving challenges of the business world.

Imagine a relay race. The success of the team depends not just on the speed of the runners but on their ability to pass the baton smoothly to each other. In the same way, effective delegation is about smoothly transferring responsibilities in a way that leverages the unique strengths of each team member, ensuring that the task progresses efficiently toward the finish line.

Empowering your team through delegation also means instilling a sense of trust. It signals to team members that their leader believes in their capabilities and values their contributions. This trust fosters a positive work environment where team members are motivated to give their best, take initiative, and contribute ideas. It creates a virtuous cycle of trust, empowerment, and high performance that drives the organization towards its goals.

By aligning tasks with the strengths and interests of team

members while providing the necessary support and fostering an environment of trust, leaders can unleash the true potential of their teams and drive productivity to new heights. This method of empowerment through delegation is a testament to the belief in the capabilities of each individual and the collective strength of the team.

Through trusting and empowering team members, distributing tasks strategically, and maximizing team potential, leaders can transform their organizations. This triad of actions is essential for engaging and motivating the team, driving innovation, and ultimately scaling the company to unparalleled success.

Trusting your team members, empowering them to take ownership, and fostering autonomy are not just leadership principles; they are the cornerstones of a thriving organization. By strategically delegating tasks, you unlock your team's potential, drive productivity, and foster a culture of innovation.

In the realm of business, where speed and precision are paramount, delegation is not just a strategy but a necessity for growth.

As a CEO, your ability to delegate effectively can determine the success trajectory of your company. It's not about relinquishing control; it's about leveraging the collective talents of your team to achieve breakthrough results.

Maximizing team potential through delegation doesn't just benefit your company internally; it also ripples outward to impact clients, stakeholders, and even underserved communities.

Embrace the power of delegation as a cutting-edge tool in your leadership arsenal, enabling you to scale your company without limits.

Putting It Into Practice: Mastering Delegation and Empowerment

Now that you understand the importance of delegation and empowerment in your journey from founder to CEO, it's time to put these principles into action. Use the following exercises and reflection prompts to cultivate your delegation skills and foster a culture of trust, autonomy, and empowerment within your organization:

1. **Assess your current delegation practices:**
- Reflect on your current approach to delegation and identify areas for improvement.
- Consider how often you delegate tasks and whether you tend to micromanage or trust your team members.
- Identify any barriers or hesitations you have when it comes to delegating responsibilities.

2. Identify your team members' strengths and interests:

- Take time to understand each team member's unique skills, experiences, and aspirations.

- Consider how you can align tasks and projects with their strengths and interests to maximize engagement and productivity.

- Have one-on-one conversations with your team members to gain insights into their goals and motivations.

3. Develop a strategic delegation plan:

- Create a list of tasks and projects that can be delegated to team members.

- Match these tasks with the appropriate team members based on their strengths and interests.

- Communicate the delegation plan clearly, outlining expectations, timelines, and resources available.

4. Foster a culture of autonomy and trust:

- Empower your team members to take ownership of their delegated tasks and make decisions independently.

- Provide the necessary resources, support, and guidance for them to succeed, but avoid micromanaging.

- Encourage open communication and regular check-ins to maintain alignment and address any challenges.

5. **Provide opportunities for growth and development:**

- Use delegation as a tool for developing your team members' skills and capabilities.
- Assign tasks that challenge them and provide opportunities for learning and growth.
- Offer regular feedback, recognition, and support to help them develop and succeed in their roles.

6. **Embrace failure as a learning opportunity:**

- Create a safe environment where team members feel comfortable taking calculated risks and learning from failures.
- Encourage a growth mindset and frame failures as opportunities for learning and improvement.
- Lead by example, sharing your own failures and the lessons you've learned from them.

7. **Continuously assess and adapt your delegation approach:**

- Regularly evaluate the effectiveness of your delegation practices and gather feedback from your team.
- Be open to adjusting your approach based on the needs and dynamics of your team and organization.
- Celebrate successes and recognize the contributions of your team members to reinforce the value of delegation and empowerment.

Remember, mastering delegation and empowerment is an ongoing journey that requires trust, communication, and a willingness to let go of control. By consistently applying these practices and making delegation a core part of your leadership strategy, you'll not only maximize your team's potential but also create a culture of ownership, innovation, and continuous growth.

Start by assessing your current delegation practices and identifying opportunities for improvement. Then, focus on understanding your team members' strengths and interests, developing a strategic delegation plan, and fostering a culture of autonomy and trust. As you progress, use delegation as a tool for developing your team members' skills and embracing failure as a learning opportunity.

By putting these principles into practice and committing to the ongoing development of your delegation skills, you'll unlock the full potential of your team and drive your organization towards unparalleled success. Embrace the power of delegation and empowerment, and watch as your leadership transforms, your team thrives, and your company scales to new heights.

Chapter 8

Strategic Planning for Success

Under the early rays of a Costa Rican sunrise, Joshua stood on the terrace of his fledgling coffee plantation, El Despertar—The Awakening. The poignant aroma of fresh beans and the gentle hum of machinery below escorted him into the burdens and hopes of a new day. Clad in a simple linen shirt that danced with the morning wind, he held in his hand a roadmap of his dreams carefully outlined on aged parchment.

He cast his gaze over the verdant slopes where coffee plants stretched toward the sun, each leaf glinting with dew. His ambition stretched with them, envisioning El Despertar as a beacon of sustainability, its name known far beyond these lush hills. A soft rustle from a nearby branch broke his contemplation. A quetzal took flight, its vibrant plumage a fleeting memory against the pale sky. Nature's beauty always had a way of anchoring his racing mind to the present.

Inside, the persistent tick of the grandfather clock gauged both time and Joshua's progress. He unfurled his roadmap, weighty objectives sprawled across the parchment-like the roots of the ancient arbol de Fuego that commanded his yard. As the espresso machine warmed up, a smooth symphony of bittersweet notes, he mused over key milestones marked in the planner—secure local partnerships, expand distribution networks, embrace eco-tourism. Market dynamics whispered of opportunities and pitfalls; adapting was survival itself.

An unexpected call, too early for pleasantries, inserted itself into the morning ritual. A trusted advisor's voice carried over the line with caution; a larger competitor had ventured into regenerative practices, possibly enticing Joshua's customers with their corporate clout. The market, much like the volcanic soil beneath his feet, was fertile but unpredictable. Unease briefly visited his heart, yet it yielded to resolve as he listened, nodded, and planned. This challenge demanded more than foresight; it called for the finesse of an eagle riding turbulent winds.

Servants began moving in the nearby kitchen, the clatter of pots and pans a reminder of lives intertwined with his venture. He made mental notes to keep close to his dedicated staff and the community that supplied them, understanding success could not bloom in isolation. A touch of boldness, a dash of diplomacy—it was a delicate balance a CEO had to maintain, a symphony he must conduct to a conclude worthy of applause.

The day surged on; meetings beckoned, and ledgers awaited his scrutiny. Yet the map remained open, its pathways and checkpoints a silent sentinel over his shoulder. The afternoon rains would soon sweep in, dressing the mountainside in mist and mystery, and Joshua welcomed the cleansing. Would he navigate his way through the storm of competition to reach the sunlit peaks of success? What new strategies would he forge in the crucible of challenge?

Unleash Your Strategic Vision

Strategic planning and execution are the pulse of every successful enterprise, setting the rhythm for growth and adaptation in a constantly evolving market landscape. For CEOs, this isn't just a task—it's an essential skill that bridges the gap between where the company stands and where it aspires to be. The journey from founder to CEO is marked by a transformational shift, emphasizing not only personal growth but also an unwavering commitment to scale your company without limits. At the core of this journey is the ability to craft a visionary yet actionable roadmap that aligns with your company's goals and the dynamic needs of the markets you serve.

Setting clear goals and developing a roadmap for success isn't just about defining what you want to achieve; it's about breaking new ground, challenging the status quo, and committing to breakthrough outcomes that will position your enterprise at the forefront of innovation. This dedication ensures that every action and decision propels your business forward, making a difference not just in your immediate environment but potentially in underserved communities and sectors craving revolutionary solutions.

Monitoring progress towards key milestones is an operation akin to navigating through uncharted waters. It requires a CEO to be both the compass and the captain—**driven by data and guided by insight**. This dual role is critical in steering your business through the challenges of changing market conditions. It's about being agile, adapting strategies in real-time, and ensuring that every team member is not only aware of the direction but is also fully engaged in the journey.

Capitalizing on opportunities for expansion is where strategic thinking and execution skills are truly tested. It's about recognizing potential before it becomes obvious to everyone else and daring to take calculated risks. Here, a CEO's role transcends business development; it becomes about **empowering leadership at all levels** and fostering an environment where innovation thrives.

Empowerment is a cornerstone of scaling any company. As a CEO, empowering your team isn't just about delegating tasks; it's about instilling a sense of ownership and commitment to the collective vision. It's about transforming your workforce into a powerhouse of strategic thinkers who are as dedicated to making a difference as you are. This empowerment leads to engaged employees who not only contribute to your company's success but also drive social innovation, pushing your enterprise to new heights.

The journey from founder to CEO is punctuated by continuous learning and an unyielding passion for excellence. It demands a commitment to not just envision success but to pursue it actively through cutting-edge strategies and bold execution. This chapter embraces the essence of strategic planning and its undeniable role in crafting a successful transition, offering insights and practical advice to help you harness the full potential of your leadership and transform your business landscape.

Embarking on this journey requires resilience and a lifelong learner's mindset. It's about broadening your horizon, continuously engaging in advanced education, and enriching your diverse educational journey. By cultivating these habits, you prepare not just yourself but your entire organization to adapt, innovate, and scale regardless of the challenges ahead.

Setting Clear Goals: The Blueprint for Success

In the realm of successful CEOs, setting clear goals stands as the foundation upon which a company's future is built. Much like an architect requires a detailed blueprint to construct a skyscraper, a CEO needs a comprehensive strategic plan to guide their company's growth. This plan starts with articulating clear, achievable goals that align with the company's mission and vision. The specificity of these goals acts as a beacon, guiding every decision and action within the organization.

Imagine navigating a dense forest without a compass. Without clear directions, the journey becomes significantly harder, and the chances of reaching the desired destination diminish. Similarly, a startup without clear goals is likely to meander through the business landscape, expending resources without making real progress. The establishment of distinct goals enables a team to move forward with purpose, aligning their efforts towards a common endpoint.

However, setting goals is only the first step. Developing a roadmap for success is what translates these goals into reality. This involves outlining strategic actions, assigning responsibilities, and setting timelines. It's about breaking down the overarching objectives into smaller, manageable tasks that collectively lead to the attainment of the main goals. This systematic approach ensures that every team member knows their role, understands the timeline, and is committed to contributing towards the company's success.

Adapting to unforeseen challenges is also a crucial component of this roadmap. Like a river that adjusts its course when encountering obstacles, a successful strategic plan incorporates flexibility, allowing the company to navigate through uncertainties and challenges without losing sight of its goals. Implementing regular review points within the plan provides opportunities to assess progress, make necessary adjustments, and remain agile in a rapidly changing business environment.

Setting clear goals and developing a roadmap for success through strategic planning is akin to plotting a course through uncharted waters. It provides direction, fosters alignment, and ensures progress towards achieving long-term success.

Navigating Towards Milestones: The Compass of Strategic Execution

Every journey to success is punctuated by milestones, markers that signify progress and achievements along the way. In the context of strategic planning, monitoring progress towards these key milestones is not only inspiring but essential. It enables CEOs and their teams to gauge the effectiveness of their strategies, celebrate wins, and recalibrate when necessary. Just as a captain uses a compass to navigate a ship, a CEO uses these milestones to steer the company in the right direction, ensuring it remains on course toward its ultimate goals.

The business landscape, much like the weather, can change rapidly and without warning. Adapting to these changes is a testament to a company's resilience and agility. This adaptability isn't just about surviving; it's about leveraging new opportunities, preempting threats, and maintaining a competitive edge. It requires a keen eye on the market, a finger on the pulse of consumer demand, and an openness to pivot strategies as needed.

Imagine a ship embarking on an ocean voyage. The captain has charted a course, but unexpected storms and shifting currents demand quick thinking and flexibility. Similarly, a company might face unexpected market shifts or competitive movements that require adjustments to the initial plan. Like the skilled captain who navigates through rough seas by adjusting the sails, a CEO must be adept at steering the company through economic fluctuations and market changes without losing sight of the destination.

Monitoring progress involves measuring performance against predefined benchmarks and milestones. This quantitative approach ensures objectivity, allowing leaders to make informed decisions. However, the qualitative aspect – understanding the 'why' behind the numbers – is equally important. It might reveal insights about market dynamics, customer behavior, or internal processes that can inform future strategies.

Regularly revisiting the strategic plan and its milestones fosters a culture of continuous improvement and learning. It encourages teams to remain engaged, focused, and committed to the shared vision, ensuring that everyone pulls in the same direction. By celebrating achievements, learning from setbacks, and staying adaptable, a company can sustain its growth momentum and scale new heights.

Could reflecting on progress and remaining adaptable in the face of change be the secret to transforming challenges into stepping stones for success?

Capitalizing on Opportunities for Expansion

In the search for growth and expansion, strategic thinking and execution are indispensable tools in a CEO's arsenal. As a CEO, you must be able to not only spot opportunities for expansion but to seize them with precision and effectiveness. Like a chess grandmaster, a CEO must anticipate moves ahead, plan strategically, and execute with precision. This foresighted approach ensures that when opportunities arise, the company is not just ready but positioned to capitalize on them.

Expansion opportunities can present themselves in various forms - entering a new market, launching a new product line, or forging strategic partnerships. The ability to recognize these opportunities is crucial, but the real challenge lies in evaluating whether they align with the company's strategic goals and capabilities. It requires a deep understanding of the company's strengths, the competitive landscape, and market trends. This strategic alignment ensures that resources are invested in ventures with the highest potential for returns.

Imagine a surfer waiting for the perfect wave. They must

choose wisely, committing only when they see one with the potential to carry them forward. Similarly, CEOs must discern which opportunities have the potential to propel the company forward and which might lead to wasted effort. This selective approach maximizes the impact of the company's efforts and resources, driving towards growth and expansion.

Culture Change Model: A Strategic Framework for Expansion

Assessment

The Culture Change Model begins with a thorough assessment of the current organizational culture. This step is akin to mapping the terrain before setting out on a journey. It involves gathering data through employee surveys, interviews, and observations, providing a comprehensive overview of the prevailing attitudes, behaviors, and norms. Understanding the starting point is crucial for plotting the course towards the desired cultural landscape.

Vision for Cultural Change

Having assessed the current culture, the next step is defining a clear vision for the desired cultural change. This vision acts as the destination on the road map of cultural transformation. It articulates the values, behaviors, and norms that the CEO and leadership team wish to instill within the organization. This vision statement becomes a rallying point for the entire company, guiding every strategy, decision, and action towards embodying these desired cultural attributes.

Leadership Alignment

Culture change begins at the top. Leadership alignment ensures that the behaviors exhibited by the company's leaders are in sync with the desired cultural shift. Leaders must model the values and behaviors they wish to see, as their actions set the tone for the rest of the organization. This alignment is crucial for building credibility and driving the culture change forward.

Reinforcement and Sustainability

The final component of the Culture Change Model focuses on embedding the new culture for the long term. This involves integrating the desired values and behaviors into every facet of the organization, from performance management to recognition programs. Continuous feedback mechanisms and adjustments ensure that the culture remains aligned with the evolving vision and goals of the company.

This model provides a structured approach to orchestrating a cultural shift within an organization. By focusing on assessment, vision, communication, leadership, and sustainability, CEOs can effectively drive the culture change needed to support expansion and long-term success.

By mastering the art of setting clear goals, monitoring progress, and seizing opportunities for expansion through strategic thinking and execution, CEOs can steer their companies toward unprecedented growth and success.

Final Thoughts

Strategic planning and execution are the cornerstones of a CEO's success. By **setting clear goals, developing a roadmap for success**, and **monitoring progress towards key milestones**, CEOs can navigate their companies towards growth and resilience. The ability to adapt to changing market conditions and seize opportunities for expansion hinges on honing these essential skills. As leaders commit to mastering strategic thinking and execution, they pave the way for sustainable business outcomes and long-term success.

This chapter has underscored the pivotal role of strategic planning in achieving breakthrough results and driving business evolution. It is through a relentless focus on **strategy, adapting to change**, and **seizing opportunities** that CEOs can position their companies as industry leaders. The power of strategic thinking lies in its capacity to propel organizations towards their envisioned future, empowering them to scale, innovate, and make a substantial impact.

In the dynamic landscape of business, the journey from founder to CEO demands a commitment to continuous improvement and a dedication to mastering the art of strategic planning. By embracing a mindset of growth and a proactive approach to navigating challenges, CEOs can unleash the full potential of their companies and themselves. Strategic planning isn't just a tool; it's a **philosophy** that guides visionary leaders towards manifesting their boldest aspirations and shaping the future of their organizations.

Putting It Into Practice: Mastering Strategic Planning for Success

Now that you understand the importance of strategic planning and its role in your journey from founder to CEO, it's time to put these principles into action. Use the following exercises and reflection prompts to cultivate your strategic thinking skills and develop a comprehensive plan for your organization's success:

1. **Conduct a SWOT analysis:**
- Identify your company's strengths, weaknesses, opportunities, and threats.
- Consider both internal factors (strengths and weaknesses) and external factors (opportunities and threats).
- Use this analysis to inform your strategic planning process.

2. **Set clear and measurable goals:**

- Define specific, measurable, achievable, relevant, and time-bound (SMART) goals for your organization.
- Ensure that these goals align with your company's mission, vision, and values.
- Break down long-term goals into shorter-term objectives and milestones.

3. **Develop a strategic roadmap:**

- Create a detailed plan outlining the steps needed to achieve your goals.
- Assign responsibilities, allocate resources, and set timelines for each step.
- Identify potential obstacles and develop contingency plans to address them.

4. **Establish key performance indicators (KPIs):**

- Determine the metrics you will use to measure progress towards your goals.
- Set targets for each KPI and regularly track your performance against these targets.
- Use data-driven insights to inform decision-making and adjust your strategy as needed.

5. **Foster a culture of continuous improvement:**

- Encourage a growth mindset within your organization, emphasizing learning and development.

- Regularly review and assess your strategic plan, making adjustments as needed based on changing circumstances or new information.
- Celebrate successes and learn from setbacks, using each experience to refine your approach.

6. **Identify and seize opportunities for expansion:**

- Continuously scan the market for potential growth opportunities, such as new markets, products, or partnerships.
- Evaluate each opportunity based on its alignment with your strategic goals and your organization's capabilities.
- Develop a clear business case and action plan for pursuing selected opportunities.

7. **Engage and empower your team:**

- Communicate your strategic vision and goals clearly to your entire organization.
- Involve team members in the strategic planning process, seeking their input and fostering a sense of ownership.
- Empower employees to take initiative and contribute to the achievement of strategic objectives.

8. **Embrace adaptability and resilience:**

- Cultivate a mindset of adaptability, remaining open to change and ready to pivot when necessary.
- Develop contingency plans and risk management strategies to navigate unexpected challenges.

- Foster a culture of resilience, encouraging your team to view setbacks as opportunities for growth and learning.

Remember, mastering strategic planning is an ongoing process that requires dedication, flexibility, and a commitment to continuous improvement. By consistently applying these practices and making strategic thinking a core part of your leadership approach, you'll position your organization for long-term success and sustainable growth.

By putting the above-mentioned principles into practice and committing to the ongoing development of your strategic planning skills, you'll unlock the full potential of your organization and drive meaningful, lasting success. Embrace the power of strategic thinking, and watch as your leadership transforms, your company thrives, and your impact grows.

Chapter 9

Mastering Emotional Intelligence

Lisa sat with quiet certainty at the corner of the long, polished conference table, the early sun casting a glow across its surface like warm honey. The shuffle of papers echoed softly in the room as his team assembled for the morning meeting. She noticed the subtle tension in their postures, the anxious darting of eyes. They felt the weight of the impending merger, a corporate alchemy that promised much but threatened the delicate balance of their work culture.

Silently, she acknowledged her own role in navigating these waters. Lisa had always prided herself on a keen emotional understanding, a skill that had endeared her to her colleagues and cemented her place as a leader. Yet now, the very humanity of her team seemed like a sea stirred by conflicting currents. She needed to harness this, to be both compass and anchor.

Mark, her assistant, moved with an efficiency that opposed his concern. He handed out the agenda, his nod toward Lisa carrying an unspoken ask for reassurance. She returned it with a smile that didn't quite reach her eyes, aware that the mood was a resource to be tended to, like the potted ferns lining the room that required just enough light and water to thrive.

As discussion unfurled like the day outside, Lisa listened to the voices of her team. Angela spoke of deadlines with an enthusiasm that bordered on panic; Tom argued about resource allocation with a heat that spoke of deeper fears. Lisa felt their emotions as clearly as the table beneath her fingers. She pondered the balance between guiding them and dictating, between the empathy that revealed their needs and the decisiveness that sometimes must eclipse it.

Through the large window, the city moved with indifferent haste, unaware of the tiny dramas within glass-paneled offices. Lisa considered how the landscape of the workplace was a microcosm of those streets below – each individual an intersection of paths, desires, and fears, all seeking a sign to point the way.

She broke in gently, steering the conversation like a patient teacher. Her tone, firm yet compassionate, suggested the calm of deep waters. "Let's remember," she said, "our strength lies in understanding not just the figures and forecasts but each other. We succeed together."

A pause settled, the shifting of papers ceased, and the team looked to Lisa. They sought certainty in a time of upheaval, a trust that their shared journey would not lead them astray. Could she, in understanding her own emotional landscape and theirs, chart a course that fulfilled both the company's goals and the human needs of those who worked within its walls?

The meeting adjourned with tasks assigned and deadlines set, yet the true work lay in the unspoken vows of understanding and empathy that Lisa carried with her. Outside, the day had blossomed fully, and the sun now held dominion over the sky, indifferent to the happenings of humankind. Jonathan stood alone in the quiet aftermath, thinking of the journey ahead.

Would the strength of their bonds weather the storms of change, or would the disruption of progress demand more than they could give?

Unlock the Power of Emotional Intelligence

Emotional intelligence is not just a catchphrase; it's a breakthrough skill set essential for those at the wheel of today's fast-paced and complex business environments. At the core of effective leadership lies the profound ability to understand, manage, and leverage emotions in positive ways to relieve stress, communicate effectively, empathize with others, overcome challenges, and defuse conflict. **The reflective impact of emotional intelligence on leadership effectiveness** cannot be overstated, making it a cornerstone for any CEO looking to scale their company without limits.

Central to mastering emotional intelligence is the awareness that one's emotional state directly influences one's ability to lead. This understanding is paramount for founders transitioning into CEO roles, as the unique challenges of scaling a business require a leader who is not only technically proficient but also emotionally intuitive. By *enhancing self-awareness and emotional regulation*, leaders can create an environment that fosters productivity, creativity, and innovation.

Building strong relationships and inspiring trust are fundamental outcomes of high emotional intelligence. Trust is the foundation of any successful relationship, and in the business context, it is the linchpin of high-performing teams. Leaders who demonstrate empathy and genuine concern for their team's well-being are better positioned to engage and motivate their workforce, cultivating a positive organizational culture that can withstand the pressures of growth and change.

Empathy and self-awareness are essential tools for relationship-building, allowing leaders to make informed, compassionate decisions that consider the feelings and perspectives of others. This empathetic approach does not mean compromising on the hard choices often required in leadership; instead, it means those decisions are communicated and executed in ways that minimize negative impact and maintain respect and dignity for all involved.

Driving team performance and achieving business goals are natural progressions from the foundation laid by solid emotional intelligence. Teams led by emotionally intelligent leaders are more cohesive, resilient, and adaptable—qualities that are indispensable in today's rapidly changing business landscape. Furthermore, leaders who prioritize emotional intelligence are better equipped to recognize and harness the diverse strengths and talents within their teams, aligning them with the organization's strategic objectives.

Lastly, for CEOs committed to making a difference—not just within their organizations but also in the broader community— emotional intelligence is a critical tool. It empowers leaders to engage with and empower underserved communities, fostering inclusivity and ensuring that their company's scaling efforts bring value to all stakeholders. The commitment to continuous learning and personal growth reflects the lifelong journey of leadership, underscoring the transformation that is possible when one prioritizes emotional intelligence in one's personal and professional development.

In essence, emotional intelligence is more than a set of skills; it is a mindset that permeates all facets of leadership, from strategic decision-making and team building to personal resilience and societal impact. By dedicating themselves to cultivating these competencies, CEOs can not only transform their businesses but also themselves, leading with confidence and creating a legacy of positive change.

Understand and Manage Your Emotions as well as Empathize With Others for Effective Leadership

Understanding and managing your own emotions is the cornerstone of emotional intelligence. It requires a deep, introspective look into your own emotional states, identifying the triggers that set off various emotions, and recognizing the impact these emotions can have on your decision-making and leadership capabilities. Being aware of your emotions allows you to navigate complex business landscapes with a steady hand, ensuring that rationale rather than fleeting emotional responses drive your decisions.

Imagine your emotions as a river flowing through the landscape of your mind. Just as a river can be calm or turbulent depending on the weather, your emotions can vary greatly under different circumstances. The key to managing this flow isn't to dam the river but to learn to navigate its currents wisely. This metaphor highlights the importance of emotional agility in leadership. By understanding your emotional landscape, you can steer your actions and reactions in a direction that is beneficial for both you and your team.

Empathy extends this understanding to others. It involves putting yourself in another's shoes, sensing their emotions, and responding appropriately. This empathetic approach fosters a supportive work environment, encouraging open communication and building trust among team members. Moreover, empathy in leadership enhances your ability to detect unspoken tensions or discomfort in your team, allowing for timely intervention to resolve issues that could impact performance.

The interplay between managing your emotions and empathizing with others forms the bedrock of effective leadership. Not only does it enable you to make more informed, balanced decisions, but it also creates a company culture where team members feel valued and understood. This dual focus on self and others paves the way for inspirational leadership that can motivate teams to greater heights of achievement.

In essence, mastering the art of understanding and managing your own emotions while empathizing with others is crucial for transformative leadership.

Build Strong Relationships, Inspire Trust, and Foster a Positive Organizational Culture Through Emotional Intelligence

Building strong relationships within your organization starts with trust, which is fostered through consistent, empathetic interactions. Emotional intelligence acts as the linchpin in this process, enabling leaders to connect with their teams on a deeper level. By showing genuine interest in the personal and professional growth of your team members, you lay the foundation for a culture of mutual respect and loyalty.

Consider the process of building trust as planting a garden. You start with the seed of emotional intelligence, which then needs to be nurtured with understanding, empathy, and consistent positive interactions. Over time, this garden grows, blossoming into strong relationships that underpin the organizational culture. Just like a well-tended garden attracts wildlife, a positive culture attracts talent, encouraging them to grow and thrive within the organization.

The ripple effect of emotional intelligence in a leadership role goes beyond just building relationships. It inspires a sense of belonging and loyalty among team members, which is critical for maintaining morale and productivity. Leaders who are adept at reading the room can tailor their communication and decisions to better align with their team's needs and aspirations, thus avoiding misunderstandings and conflicts that could derail progress.

Fostering a positive organizational culture is another aspect where emotional intelligence shines. It allows leaders to create an environment where employees feel safe to express ideas, fail, learn, and innovate. This culture of openness and inclusivity is a breeding ground for creative solutions and breakthroughs, setting the stage for the company's long-term success.

The impact of emotional intelligence on leadership effectiveness, therefore, cannot be overstated. By fostering strong relationships, inspiring trust, and nurturing a positive organizational culture, leaders equipped with emotional intelligence set their teams and companies up for unparalleled success.

Drive Team Performance and Achieve Business Goals by Cultivating Empathy, Self-Awareness, and Relationship-Building Skills

Driving team performance towards achieving business goals requires more than just strategic understanding; it requires a leader to be attuned to the emotional needs and dynamics of their team. Cultivating empathy allows you to understand and appreciate your team members' perspectives, leading to better communication and collaboration. This understanding fosters a conducive environment for high performance and innovation.

Transformational leaders recognize that each team member brings unique skills, experiences, and perspectives to the table. Their role is to harness these individual strengths and create an environment where team members can collaborate effectively towards a common goal. This is achieved through empathy, self-awareness, and strong relationship-building skills.

Empathy allows leaders to understand and respond to the needs and emotions of their team members. By actively listening and demonstrating genuine concern, leaders can build trust and foster a sense of belonging within the team. This emotional intelligence also enables leaders to navigate complex interpersonal dynamics and resolve conflicts constructively.

Self-awareness is another critical component of transformational leadership. Leaders who are attuned to their own strengths, weaknesses, and biases can make more informed decisions and adapt their leadership style to suit the needs of their team. This introspection also allows leaders to model the kind of self-reflection and personal growth they wish to see in their team members.

Finally, transformational leaders excel at building strong relationships with their team members. They take the time to get to know each individual, their aspirations, and their challenges. By investing in these relationships, leaders can provide personalized support, guidance, and opportunities for development. This not only enhances individual performance but also contributes to a positive team culture where everyone feels valued and motivated to give their best.

The relationship-building aspect is what ties everything together. By building strong, trust-based relationships with team members, leaders can create a highly motivated team that is committed to achieving the company's goals. This entails recognizing and valuing the diverse talents and contributions of each team member, encouraging open dialogue, and providing support and resources needed for success.

By intertwining empathy, self-awareness, and relationship-building, leaders pave the way for enhanced team performance and the achievement of strategic business goals.

Mastering Emotional Intelligence

Emotional intelligence stands as a cornerstone of effective leadership. It is not merely a soft skill but a critical competency that propels CEOs to new heights of success. **Understanding and managing emotions**, coupled with the ability to **empathize with others**, form the bedrock upon which remarkable leadership is built. This chapter has underscored the revolutionary impact of emotional intelligence on leadership effectiveness, emphasizing the pivotal role of **empathy, self-awareness, and relationship-building** in steering teams toward unparalleled performance and actualizing ambitious business objectives.

By committing to honing their emotional intelligence, CEOs can **forge robust relationships**, instill trust effortlessly, and cultivate a workplace culture poised for brilliance. The cutting-edge insights shared here have shed light on how emotional intelligence plays a pivotal role in not just business success but in transforming organizational dynamics from within. This chapter has unveiled the power of emotional intelligence in **driving team performance**, outlining a path where empathy, self-awareness, and relationship-building synergize to propel businesses toward unparalleled heights.

Celebrating the essence of emotional intelligence is not merely a call to action but a testament to the fundamental shift it brings in how leaders engage with their teams, foster collaboration, and steer their companies towards unfathomed success. **Embrace emotional intelligence as your ultimate tool**, master it like a seasoned artisan, and watch as your leadership journey transforms before your very eyes.

Putting It Into Practice: Cultivating Emotional Intelligence

Now that you understand the significance of emotional intelligence in your journey from founder to CEO, it's time to put these insights into practice. Use the following exercises and reflection prompts to develop your emotional intelligence and apply it to your leadership approach:

1. **Practice self-awareness:**
- Set aside time each day for introspection and self-reflection.
- Pay attention to your emotions and how they influence your thoughts, decisions, and behaviors.
- Identify your strengths and weaknesses, and consider how they impact your leadership style.

2. **Develop emotional regulation:**
- When faced with challenging situations, take a step back and assess your emotional response.
- Practice techniques such as deep breathing, mindfulness, or cognitive reframing to manage your emotions effectively.
- Reflect on past experiences where you successfully regulated your emotions and apply those lessons to future situations.

3. **Cultivate empathy:**
- Actively listen to your team members and seek to understand their perspectives and emotions.

- Put yourself in their shoes and consider how your decisions and actions may impact them.
- Show genuine concern for their well-being and offer support when needed.

4. **Build strong relationships:**

- Invest time in getting to know your team members on a personal level.
- Foster open communication and encourage feedback, creating a safe space for honest dialogue.
- Recognize and celebrate the achievements and contributions of your team members.

5. **Lead with authenticity:**

- Be transparent about your own emotions and vulnerabilities when appropriate.
- Admit mistakes and show a willingness to learn and grow from them.
- Align your actions with your values and lead by example.

6. **Foster a positive organizational culture:**

- Create an environment that values emotional intelligence, empathy, and collaboration.
- Encourage a growth mindset and provide opportunities for personal and professional development.
- Celebrate diversity and inclusivity, recognizing the strengths that different perspectives bring to the team.

7. **Seek feedback and continuously improve:**

- Regularly ask for feedback from your team members, peers, and mentors on your emotional intelligence and leadership effectiveness.
- Embrace constructive criticism as an opportunity for growth and development.
- Commit to ongoing learning and self-improvement, staying open to new ideas and approaches.

Remember, developing emotional intelligence is a lifelong journey that requires consistent practice and self-reflection. By integrating these exercises into your daily routine and making emotional intelligence a priority in your leadership approach, you'll create a transformative impact on your team, your organization, and your own personal growth.

Start by focusing on self-awareness and emotional regulation, as these form the foundation of emotional intelligence. As you become more adept at managing your own emotions, extend your focus to cultivating empathy and building strong relationships with your team members. Lead with authenticity and foster a positive organizational culture that values emotional intelligence and collaboration.

By putting these principles into practice and committing to ongoing self-improvement, you'll unlock the full potential of your leadership and drive your organization toward extraordinary success. Embrace the power of emotional intelligence, and watch as your team flourishes, your company thrives, and your impact as a leader grows exponentially.

Chapter 10

The 12-Week Framework to Business Growth

In the cool dimness of her new office, Ava pressed her fingertips against the mahogany desk's surface, feeling the weight of invisible shareholders and the burden of expectations that now sought to reside upon her shoulders. The role of CEO had sounded sweet in the echo chamber of ambition, but reality painted starker contrasts. Transition whispered change, a transformation she was to undergo in twelve short weeks.

Her gaze settled on the spine of a book perched on the shelf, 'CEO Evolution.' Its presence was not a matter of luck but a prescription, a roadmap to morphing founder passion into CEO strategy while maintaining the company's prosperous beat. Ava let her eyes close, allowing her thoughts to spiral back to her early firebrand days, where it had all been about the chase, the creation. Now, those dreams demanded a seasoned hand to guide them.

The click of the door broke her reflections. Her assistant's voice offered a tether, "Your 2 PM wants a word now. " Ava nodded, her mind a cauldron of conjecture. Would these strategies really sculpt her into the leader her company deserved?

Outside, the city hummed, unconcerned, as the sun began its descent, casting long orange fingers through the blinds. Ava stood silhouetted, her silhouette contrasting against the fading light, symbolic of a vision transitioning yet tenacious.

In another corner, staff chattered, their words snippets of daily trials and triumphs. Ava inhaled their industrious hum. It was these moments, these people, for whom her evolution was non-negotiable. Was the structured framework enough, she wondered, to reinvent not just herself but the company's culture?

She trailed her fingers across the titles of other books, imbued with promise and wisdom. Desks away, keyboards clacked, and the scent of activity was almost palpable. Ava turned, facing the horizon where the city met the sky, contemplation stitched into the furrows of her brow. Was the leap from founder to CEO merely about personal growth, or did the destiny of countless others weaved into her company's tapestry hinge on her willingness to step into broader daylight and deeper shadows?

What if the real transformation was not in reaching the quarter's goals but in embracing the vulnerability of not knowing, the boldness in seeking, and the fortitude of growing, all contained within the span of a heartbeat or a 12-week quarter? Could the CEO she would become shape the world just as it had shaped her?

Your Blueprint to Transformative Leadership and Explosive Growth

The journey from a visionary entrepreneur to an effective CEO is fraught with challenges, yet it is essential for scaling a business beyond its initial success. Chapters 2 to 9 in this book are a practical 12-week roadmap designed to facilitate this critical transition. This guide is not just about business growth; it's about personal transformation. The core of this evolution centers on mastering a structured framework for sustainable company growth, undergoing significant mindset shifts, and honing essential leadership skills. These elements are not merely suggestions but fundamental principles that, when applied diligently, promise tangible results in just three months.

Your chrysalis from entrepreneur to CEO is a process that demands commitment, a willingness to learn, and an openness to evolve. It goes beyond conventional business development strategies, pushing you to engage deeply with your personal development. This chapter synthesizes the essence of this process, elaborating on how to align personal growth with business goals strategically. The essence of leadership lies in continuous learning and adapting, and this is your guide to becoming a lifelong learner who leads a cutting-edge business to new heights.

Emphasizing strategy, leadership, and scaling offers insights and practical advice for ambitious founders ready to step into a CEO role. It outlines a clear path to not only adapting to but also embracing the responsibilities and challenges that come with being at the helm of a growing business. This transition is crucial for entrepreneurs who have mastered the art of starting a company but now need to learn how to scale it effectively without limits.

The 12-week framework is not just a set of instructions; it's a journey of transformation. It is about integrating strategic thinking with personal growth, embodying the leadership qualities needed to inspire a team, and implementing breakthrough strategies to ensure your business not only grows but thrives. This period of intensive growth focuses on actionable steps to engage and empower your team, reach untapped markets, and make a significant impact.

The Intersection of Personal and Business Growth

Implementing the strategies outlined here will unlock your potential, empower you to lead with confidence, and remove the limits on your company's growth. It's about creating a synergy between your personal development as a leader and the evolution of your business. This alignment is critical in driving sustainable growth, fostering innovation, and engaging underserved communities in meaningful ways. The roadmap outlined applies to diverse industries and is designed to be flexible, acknowledging that every business—and its leader—is unique.

A Commitment to Making a Difference

Engaging with this process means committing to a significant shift in how you view both your role and your business. It's about moving from being operationally involved in every detail to adopting a strategic mindset that focuses on scalable growth. This requires not only a deep understanding of your business and its potential but also an unwavering dedication to your personal development as a leader. The strategies emphasize the importance of making a difference—not just in your company but in the broader community and industry you serve.

From Theory to Action: Strategy, Leadership, and Growth

What sets this guide apart is its foundation in actionable strategies. It champions innovative thinking, strategic planning, and the courageous leadership necessary to transform challenges into opportunities for growth. By the end of these 12 weeks, equipped with new insights and skills, you will not only see a tangible difference in your business but also feel a profound shift in your capabilities and mindset as a leader.

In extracting the essence of transformation from founder to CEO, the journey outlined offers more than a path to scaling your business. It represents a leap towards creating a sustainable impact and forging a legacy that transcends the bottom line. As you navigate these transformative waters, remember that growth is a continuous journey, one that demands a commitment to innovation, leadership, and making a difference. The time to start this journey is now, with the tools, strategies, and insights provided here serving as your compass toward becoming a CEO who leads with confidence and propels your business to unprecedented heights.

Transitioning from the role of a founder to a CEO is akin to growing a plant from seed – both processes require structure, care, and the right conditions to thrive. Just as a gardener needs to follow certain guidelines to ensure the healthy growth of their plant, founders need a structured framework to evolve into effective CEOs. This evolution is crucial for driving sustainable growth within their companies. A structured approach not only provides clarity and direction but also helps in navigating the complexities of scaling a business.

One critical element of this framework involves setting clear goals and developing a roadmap to achieve them. This process includes identifying key growth metrics, establishing short-term and long-term objectives, and assigning responsibilities. Just as a gardener plans out the space where each plant will grow, determines the right amount of sunlight and water, and schedules planting and harvest times, a CEO must plan how to allocate resources effectively, monitor progress, and adjust strategies as needed.

Another aspect of the framework focuses on cultivating a strong organizational culture and building a cohesive team. This part of the process involves hiring the right people who share the vision of the company, developing a strong internal communication system, and creating a culture where feedback and continuous improvement are valued. It's similar to ensuring that the soil is fertile and that plants are compatible with each other, supporting rather than hindering growth.

Lastly, the framework emphasizes the importance of personal growth and leadership development. Just as a plant needs the right environment to grow, founders need to develop themselves into leaders who can inspire, motivate, and lead their teams effectively. This includes learning how to manage stress, make tough decisions, and communicate effectively. Leadership development is an ongoing process, requiring founders to be receptive to feedback, willing to learn, and committed to self-improvement.

By following a structured framework, founders can smoothly transition to effective CEOs and drive sustainable growth in their companies.

Practice Mindset Shifts and Essential Leadership Skills

Transforming into an effective CEO requires not just strategic planning and operational prowess but also a significant shift in mindset. This transformation is driven by the realization that what worked at the seed stage of the business might not be as effective when scaling. Entrepreneurs need to transition from a hands-on approach to a more strategic role, focusing on leadership, vision, and the capacity to guide their team towards achieving company goals.

The practice of mindset shifts involves redefining one's identity from being the sole problem-solver to empowering others to solve problems. This includes fostering a culture of trust where mistakes are viewed as learning opportunities. Picture a ship's captain who doesn't steer every wave but trusts the crew and navigates the course. Similarly, CEOs need to trust their teams, delegate effectively, and focus on steering the organization's strategic direction.

Developing essential leadership skills is as crucial as mindset shifts. Leaders must hone their ability to communicate effectively, both in casting the vision and in the day-to-day interactions that affirm the value of each team member. They need to inspire and motivate, recognizing that each word spoken is like a brush stroke in the broader picture of company culture. Balancing empathy with decisiveness, negotiation skills with authenticity, and resilience with vulnerability becomes the art and science of effective leadership.

Moreover, tangible results within the 12-week timeframe are achievable through the consistent application of these mindset shifts and leadership skills. Like an athlete preparing for a competition, leaders must set clear goals, follow through with disciplined practice, and seek feedback for continuous improvement. It's a process of building muscle memory for leadership—the more you practice, the more natural these skills become.

Implementing feedback mechanisms and measuring progress are critical in assessing the impact of these changes. This may involve setting up regular check-ins with team members, soliciting feedback from customers, or conducting self-assessments to gauge leadership effectiveness. This ongoing assessment ensures that the journey of transformation remains on track and adjusts as necessary.

Could discovering and cultivating your hidden strengths be the key to unlocking unparalleled growth in your business and leadership journey?

Unlock Your Potential and Lead with Confidence

To truly unlock one's potential and lead a business to scale without limits, it's imperative to implement the strategies outlined with commitment and conviction. It's like navigating a boat in open waters, having a detailed map and a strong compass—where the map represents the strategies outlined and the compass, your internal drive and confidence, guiding you through uncharted territories.

Starting with self-awareness sets the foundation for unlocking potential. It involves a deep dive into understanding your strengths, weaknesses, and unique leadership style. Like recognizing the unique properties of different materials when constructing a building, understanding your intrinsic qualities enables you to leverage your strengths optimally and work on areas that need improvement.

Leading with confidence then naturally follows. Confidence in this context does not mean an absence of doubt but rather the assurance in your ability to make decisions and the resilience to face challenges head-on. It's about believing in your capacity to navigate the business through growth phases, much like a captain's belief in their ability to steer their ship through storms.

Scaling your business involves a holistic approach, encompassing strategic planning, team development, and innovation. It's comparable to overseeing a vast, thriving city—

where meticulous planning, resource allocation, and continuous development ensure its growth and sustainability. Innovation mainly, plays a pivotal role in scaling. By encouraging a culture of innovation within your team, you foster an environment where creative solutions and breakthrough ideas flourish, propelling the business forward.

By embracing a structured growth framework, shifting your mindset, and honing your leadership skills, you unlock your potential, lead with confidence, and scale your business beyond limits.

Reflecting on the Journey

Throughout the course of this book, you've embarked on a transformative 12-week journey to transition from founder to CEO. By following a structured roadmap for business growth, practicing essential leadership skills, and embracing mindset shifts, you've laid the foundation for sustainable success.

Empowering Your Potential

Unlocking your potential is not just a concept but a reality to be embraced. By honing your skills, adopting a CEO mindset, and implementing the strategies outlined, you have the power to lead with confidence and drive your business towards limitless growth.

Driving Towards Success

The evolution from founder to CEO is not merely a title change; it signifies a profound shift in how you approach your role and your company. By committing to continuous learning, embracing challenges with tenacity, and driving innovation, you are positioning yourself at the forefront of your industry, poised for remarkable achievements.

Elevating Your Impact

Your journey toward becoming a CEO is evidence of your dedication and drive to make a difference. By implementing *cutting-edge strategies* and leveraging your newfound leadership skills, you are not only scaling your business but also empowering those around you and engaging with underserved communities to create a meaningful impact.

Continuing the Growth

As you move forward, remember that the path to CEO evolution is a continuous one. Stay committed to your growth, remain open to new ideas, and lead with a passion for making a difference. Your journey from founder to CEO is a testament to your resilience, determination, and unwavering belief in your ability to achieve greatness.

Embrace the Journey

The road from founder to CEO is not always easy, but it is undeniably rewarding. By embodying the principles outlined in this book and embracing the transformation with an open mind, you are setting yourself up for a future filled with possibilities, growth, and unparalleled success. Your journey is just beginning, and the best is yet to come.

Epilogue

Embarking on a Journey of Transformation and Growth

As we draw this exploration to a close, it's crucial to reflect on the potent blend of passion, innovation, and strategy that distinguishes a successful transition from a founder to a transformative CEO. Hopefully, this book can be your compass in navigating the undulating terrain of business growth, providing not just direction but a beacon of light guiding you towards becoming a leader who is not only committed to scaling their company but also dedicated to personal development and making a difference in the world.

The principles and strategies outlined in these chapters are not just theoretical musings but are the distillation of cutting-edge research, breakthrough innovations, and real-world applications. They are designed to empower you, the driven entrepreneur, to unlock your potential, engage with your teams and customers on a deeper level, and scale your company beyond limits you may have thought impossible.

Throughout our journey, we've tackled the challenges of maintaining a vibrant company culture amidst rapid growth, the art of managing time and priorities in an ever-evolving business landscape, and the science of building and leading high-performing teams. We've wrestled with making tough decisions under uncertainty, handling the stress and burnout that comes with the territory, and adapting to change with agility and foresight. Most importantly, we've honed our abilities in effective communication and influence, underlining the importance of conveying the vision and executing strategic plans with precision.

To put what you've learned into action, remember that transformation starts with small, consistent steps. Take the time to reflect on your current leadership style and mindset, identifying areas for growth and development. Engage with your team, seeking their feedback and fostering an environment of continuous improvement. Reflect on your company's strategic vision regularly and adjust your course as needed, staying true to your core values but flexible in your approach.

While this book aims to provide a comprehensive guide to your transformation from founder to CEO, it is by no means exhaustive. The landscape of business and leadership is continually evolving, and thus, **a lifelong dedication to learning and growth is essential.** There may be areas not covered in depth within these pages, which could provide fertile ground for further research or exploration. Engaging with other thought leaders, pursuing advanced education, and seeking mentorship can provide additional insights and deepen your understanding.

As you venture forth, let this book serve not just as a manual but as a source of inspiration. You are capable of remarkable transformation and equipped to scale your company and impact without limits. Let your commitment to social innovation, passion for making a difference, and pledge to empower underserved communities fuel your journey ahead.

Let this journey transform not just your business but you. As you step into your role with confidence, remember that leadership is not just about reaching destinations but about the impact you make along the way. May your path be one of growth, breakthroughs, and revolutionary success.

"To lead people, walk beside them . . . As for the best leaders, the people do not notice their existence. When the best leader's work is done, the people say, 'We did it ourselves!'"

– Lao Tzu

www.ingramcontent.com/pod-product-compliance
Lightning Source LLC
Chambersburg PA
CBHW071406120626
46546CB00002B/838